OUT OF YOUR HANDS

What Palmistry Reveals About Your Personality & Destiny

BELETA GREENAWAY

HAMPTON ROADS

Cover and interior design by Kathryn Sky-Peck
Cover illustration created using imagery from INTERFOTO / Alamy Stock Photo
Illustrations © Malcolm Wright, Beleta Greenaway, and Sasha Fenton
Typeset in Sabon

Hampton Roads Publishing Company, Inc.
Charlottesville, VA 22906
Distributed by Red Wheel/Weiser, LLC
www.redwheelweiser.com

Sign up for our newsletter and special offers by going to
www.redwheelweiser.com/newsletter.

ISBN: 978-1-64297-000-5

Library of Congress Cataloging-in-Publication Data available upon request.

Printed in Canada
MAR
10 9 8 7 6 5 4 3 2 1

I dedicate this book to Catherine Coverdale.
Thank you for your endless patience, help and support.
You truly are a very special friend.

Many thanks to Sasha Fenton for her input and help in
making this book possible, but above all for
having faith in my palmistry knowledge.

A special mention to Lynn Seal,
a fabulous palmist whose ideas have been an inspiration to me.

A big thank you to my husband, John Greenaway,
for his love and support.

Contents

Part Five: Special Markings

Part Six: Out of Your Hands

part one

PALMISTRY BASICS

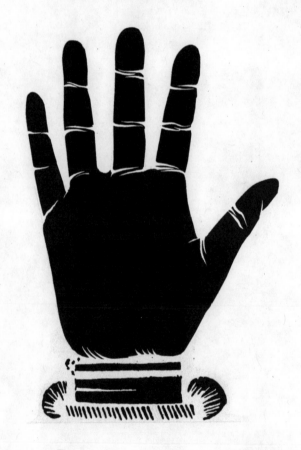

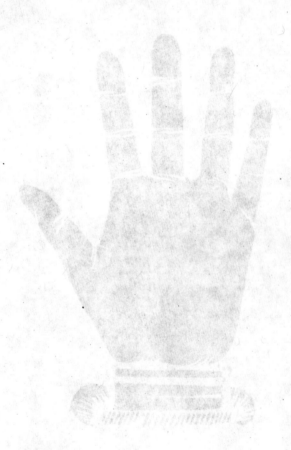

1

Reading the Map of Life

Since the beginning of human history, the hand has enthralled and captivated all cultures and races. In addition to the Indians, the Chinese, Greeks and Persians were among the first civilizations openly to practice the art of Chirology, while the Egyptians were also known to have an avid interest in it, often combining palmistry with astrology. Judging by the number of painted hand pictures found in prehistoric caves, especially in France, Spain, and Australia, it's apparent that some form of hand reading has been around since the beginning of time.

Chirology is another name for palmistry, or a study of the hands, and it probably originated in the Indian subcontinent; there are texts in Indian museums that go back over 5,000 years. However, written evidence doesn't always survive, so there may have been earlier texts than these, and an oral tradition that goes back even further.

The chances are that palmistry, along with many other esoteric skills, moved westward as a result of the Crusades, which brought Westerners into close contact with Eastern countries and peoples. Later, palmistry became associated with gypsies and then fortune tellers.

Nomadic wanderers have brought their knowledge to many parts of Europe over the last three hundred years, and the old saying "cross my palm with silver" is quite probably the origin of paying for a reading.

As mentioned, there are references to palmistry in many ancient books ranging from the Bible to the Brahmanic Vedas and the Torah.

Sadly, palmistry was forced to go underground by the Catholic Church, which labelled the craft as the work of the devil. Those who were found to be practicing chiromancy were in danger of being murdered and disposed of secretly. Despite this, man's fascination with the hand flourished, and today, all over the world, there are people who still use this magical art, with many more eager to learn the skills.

The Journey of Life

Every time you look at the lines on someone's hand, you are looking at that person's journey of life and the map of their character and fate. Although palmistry is considered a science and each line on the palm represents a certain meaning, it is also known to be another channel for psychics to gain information, because touching or feeling the hand brings a vibration to the clairvoyant and thus becomes a form of psychometry. A true clairvoyant will be able to tune into the psychic vibration of their client (sometimes called the "Querent") when performing hand analysis, thus benefiting from both psychic and scientific aspects. Sometimes an initial letter will be clearly seen on the hand, and this can represent someone very important with that initial in their name, due to come into the life of the seeker. It could be a lover, a child, or a member of the seeker's family or friends. A house or an image might suddenly appear on the palm to give the palmist extra help in defining what is going on in that person's life. Another time, you might delve into the same hand and find that particular information has gone, which means the situation has passed.

Once, I was browsing the hand of a new client and saw the image of a tepee. I asked him if he had recently been to a North American Indian reservation. His head shot up in amazement as he had just returned from one the week before.

The Romany gypsies believe that the left hand is what God has given you and the right hand is what you do with the potential. In their readings, many modem chirologists will tell you that the left hand represents the past and that it can hold karmic knowledge of previous lives, while the right hand holds knowledge of the future. Of course, this assumes the person is right-handed, because, if the person is left handed, the process is reversed.

Those who might want to become palmists will find the following lists helpful:

The Ten Do's and Don'ts of Palmistry

Do ...

1. Find a calm and peaceful room for the consultation.

2. Set the mood by burning oil or incense of lavender or poppy "opium." These two fragrances can enhance psychic ability and create a peaceful ambiance.

3. Ensure that the readings are on a one-to-one basis.

4. Have a lamp or small spotlight on the table to illuminate gloomy days.

5. Purchase a good magnifying glass to see tiny lines. Some have a light included.

6. You might wish to have your favorite crystal nearby on the table.

7. Remember your client is the most important person during their reading.

8. Practice on friends and family, inking their handprints to study. A good photocopy of their hand can be helpful if you want to avoid the mess of the ink.

9. Wash your hands before and after every consultation. You may prefer a medical hand gel. You might find that each person will have his or her own special vibration or energy, and with practice, you could link into this.

10. Turn off all telephones and try not to interrupt the reading, as that stems the flow.

Don't ...

1. Have radios or TVs playing in the room that you work in while you're giving a consultation.

2. Have children or pets running around when working.

3. Make any hair-raising predictions.

4. Become a "party piece." People will love to ask you to dinner

and bombard you with questions. I once arrived to have dinner with a new "friend" and found she had invited four of her friends as well, and I was the unwitting entertainment for the evening!

5. Be put off about making a recording of your reading for a client. Many get comfort from them, but others have bad memories.

6. NEVER read for a strange man if you are a female and if you are alone in the house. You might be asking for trouble. A few years ago, I did a full hour reading for a young man who sat in captivated silence. After the reading, he pounced on me! Luckily, I manage to throw him out on the street. It is best to ask a friend or a family member to be around if needed.

7. Discuss your private life with your client. This is extremely unprofessional and could add weight to their burdens, as well as making you vulnerable to con artists.

8. Ever divulge information from other people's readings. Every reading must be in complete and utter confidence. Remember, you will hold many secrets and often will read for large families, celebrities, and folk in all professional walks of life.

9. Be fazed by the variety of clientele you may meet, and be prepared to be flexible in your outlook. Treat everyone equally.

10. Ever discuss or criticize other well-known clairvoyants to your clients. This is extremely unprofessional. Many people visit many different psychics for fun and entertainment, and you can bet your life that anything you say will be repeated.

However, after all of the do's and don'ts, do remember to enjoy your newfound hobby or career.

Vocabulary Reminders

Chirology is: Palmistry
Palmistry is: The technique of reading hands
Chirognomy is: The study of hand shapes, finger formations, and the textures of the skin
Chiromancy is: Reading the lines on the palms

Tools of the Trade

Large Magnifying Glass

Buy the largest one you can find and ensure that it is good quality. There are some nice ones with battery lighting attached that will help to make the lines even more visible, especially on dimly lit days or dark evenings. If possible, keep it stored in a velvet pouch or bag when not in use, because the glass can easily become scratched. Keep a soft cloth in the bag to polish the glass every now and again.

Small Halogen Lamp

I find this useful when doing evening party readings, or you might prefer a small flashlight.

Fine Pens

There are times when you will want to point out clearly a line or mark on your client's hand, so a fine pointed, felt tipped pen can be used to trace the lines.

Taking Prints

You will need the following items:

- A tube of water-based printing ink. The usual color to use is black, but you may prefer another dark color. As a last resort, you can use a dark lipstick to cover the hands. It is messy, but can have excellent results if you're careful not to smudge the print. I have seen other palmists use acrylic paint quite successfully, too.

- An old plate, tray, or tile for spreading the ink out evenly.

- A small roller, a small sponge paint roller, or a cosmetic sponge.

- White paper or thin card stock.

- Paper towel or newspaper.

The Method

Place the white paper or card stock onto a paper towel or some newspaper. Squeeze a small amount of ink onto the plate and roll it until you get a good flat consistency on the roller. Roll the ink onto the palm, fingers, and thumb, making sure the wrist area (rascettes) are also inked, because they hold vital information. A cosmetic sponge can be used to dab the hand all over to make the ink even. You may wish to take several prints for each client, with some showing one area of the hand and others showing different areas.

Place the client's hand centrally on the paper and gently press down on each finger, putting light pressure on the phalanges. Try not to smudge or smear the print, as you will need it as clean as possible. Next press the inner palm down firmly, and also use the same procedure for the rascettes. If the palm is very hollow, take a folded square of paper towel and place it under the portion of paper covering the hollow part of the palm.

To get a good print of the rascettes, gently lift the fingers and palm up, ask your client slowly to roll the wrist from side to side to cover all of the lines. You might decide to do the rascettes independently on a separate piece of paper. Ink the percussion (the side of the hand opposite the thumb) up to the top edge of the Mercury finger and gently roll this area from side to side on the paper to get full coverage. It is a good idea to do the fingerprints separately as well as the full print.

When you have a full set of hand prints completed, draw carefully around the fingers and hand shape with a medium felt-tipped pen, name and date it and leave it to dry for about an hour. It is a good idea to photocopy the print as a back up. Placing it in a plastic folder will protect it from any harm.

If you decide not to have an ink print and prefer a photocopy print, make sure you don't press the hand down too hard in the photocopier, as you will get white, featureless marks. You might find you need help to get your own print done and make sure you also copy the back of the hand to see the nails as they offer a great deal of information on health issues. Many palmists will use color photocopying as well as the traditional black and white.

2

Hand Shape

Begin by looking at the hand overall, and start by noting the shape of the hand. There are four major hand shapes:

- Air
- Earth
- Fire
- Water

Novice palmists often become mystified when they try to match the hand shape with the birth sign of the individual because it doesn't always follow. For instance, I was born under the sign of Aquarius, which is an air sign, but I have a fire hand. My advice when judging personalities from palm readings is to concentrate solely on the hand shape as this seems to be the most accurate.

The Air Hand—
the Philosophical Hand

The palm is square and a little shorter than the fingers. There will be plenty of lines present in the palm. The skin texture is usually smooth and firm.

Meaning

Air palm people love company, so socializing will be at the top of their agenda.

They have many different types of friends and they can change like a chameleon to accommodate them all. They are deep thinking intellectuals who love animals and who want to put right the injustices of the world. You might find them working for good causes that will help mankind. These individuals have methodical and tidy minds, but this isn't always reflected in the way they keep their home or offices. They love detail, delight in research and history, and their intellect is usually superior to others. As their nature is all about reflection and deliberation, they won't be rushed into anything.

In love

The air hand person will want lots of communication from their partner as well as sex. Although their libido is quite high, friendship will be more important in the long run.

Negative traits

At times these types will be opinionated and nitpick about everything. Because they are so critical and can be scathing, they are hard to live with. They often have a chip on their shoulders. Sometimes they can be cold and calculating and will often play mind games.

The Earth Hand—the Practical Hand

The palm is square, with stocky fingers and a firm skin texture. The palm and fingers are both short. As a rule there will be fewer lines on this type of hand than the other types.

Meaning

Earth hand people are dependable, stoic, and hard working, and their feet are planted firmly on the ground. If they are in repetitive work, they won't mind too much and they will put in lots of effort. They have a truly honest personality and believe in fair play. If I were to employ someone, then this type of hand would be the one I would choose because its owner will be very conscientious in all they do. The earth hand person will love to be out of doors; they often grow their own vegetables and have a sense of pride in providing for the family. When they retire, many seek solitude in the country and perhaps will own a farm with chickens, ducks, and geese. They also love cats and dogs, so they could end up with a bit of a menagerie.

In love

Earth hand owners are romantic. They love sex and won't have many inhibitions. They adore food, soft lights and drawn curtains, a fine bottle of wine, and a good film on the television. If they can cuddle up with their chosen companion for the evening, they will be perfectly happy and content.

Negative traits

These people are stubborn and can be ill at ease or gauche in company. Some are often tongue-tied and shy. If their mind is fixed on something, then they will be blinded to all persuasion, especially if the thumb is broad and stout.

The Fire Hand—the Artistic Hand

The palm should be considerably longer than the fingers, and there will be plenty of lines on the palm. Often the color will be slightly rosier than other hand types and the hand will be warm to the touch. A good fire hand will have a bold Mount of Venus and a strong Mars Mount.

Meaning

These people are on the ball and are good judges of character. They live for the moment and gain what they can as it comes along. Fire hands are psychic and can read minds, so you need to guard your thoughts from them. Their motto is carpe diem . . . seize the day.

Owners of this hand are usually very active types who love excitement and action. Fun loving and enthusiastic, they enjoy exploring. They will prefer to be the boss and will frequently run their own businesses. The fire hand types will be artistic and warm hearted and will rely on their intuition.

In love

When in love, fire hand people can be ardent and have a high libido. In the bedroom, they can be inventive and will find sex toys and saucy videos a hoot. The male owner of a fire hand will often laugh his lady into bed. Before getting married, they will have quite a few partners, but when they settle down they will be very loyal.

Negative traits

Fire hands can be noisy and rush from one thing to another, expending their energies on trivia. As they can sometimes be overbearing and attention-seeking, they lack real friendships and often end up lonely.

The Water Hand—the Psychic Hand

The palm is long, as are the fingers. Some say this is the most psychic of all hands. There will be myriad lines in the palm, which can be a nightmare for the palmist when trying to analyze it.

Meaning

Water hand owners are dreamy, mysterious and psychic. The phases of the Moon can affect them and the moon mount will be well developed on this type of hand. The Neptune mount should be rounded, too. Water hands show good creative abilities and these people make wonderful friends and great parents.

In love

As they are dreamy, they will love the formality of courtship, poetry, and long romantic walks in the countryside. Secret trysts and romantic letters appeal to them. Often they are too romantic and vulnerable. Their high ideals will often come crashing around them, ultimately causing heartbreak.

Negative traits

Water hands can be possessive, manipulative, and revengeful. They never forget past hurts. Indeed they never forget anything!

Mixed Hands

Often one will come across a hand that does not fit into the four categories. The left hand might be fire and the right hand might be earth. If the person is right-handed, then you should use the character in the left hand for the past personality and the right hand for the future development. Sometimes the hand shapes vary so much that no decision can be made, and you will have to look at other factors on the palm to help you. In time, experience will give you a feel for what is right.

Meaning

This character will be multi-talented, a jack-of-all-trades and they will most likely have several careers. They can be witty, quick thinking, and very astute.

In love

I have found mixed hand types can be quite promiscuous. They like variation and can be in love with two or three people at the same time. Their restless nature can prevent long and lasting relationships. On the plus side, because of their sexual experiences, they make very good lovers.

Negative traits

They can be like will-o'-the-wisps, unable to settle down and end up drifting from one place to another. They rarely finish a project and can be a nightmare for partners, as they will constantly want to move and change jobs.

Fingers and Palms the Same Length

When this formation is present, the person will be well balanced, reliable, and level headed. They enjoy studying and work, but will also like time away from employment. Being adaptable, they often have a variety of careers during their lifetime and are usually successful in all of them. They have a brilliant sense of humor and because of that, they are popular.

Broad Palms

These types are very loving and steady, especially in marriage. They are "older souls" and so have great wisdom, sympathy, and depth. Broad palm people are popular and others seek their advice. They choose roles to help society, and if they have the Medical Striata on their hands (see the chapter on minor lines), could become doctors, nurses, or some kind of health practitioners.

They have energy, drive, and ambition but also like to please others. If children have broad palms, they are rarely naughty and will sometimes seem older than their years.

Narrow Palms

This type of palm can sometimes belong to narrow-minded people. The owner will find it hard to be generous. If they are to purchase a gift for someone, they will look for a bargain, while at the same time treating themselves to something expensive. Some narrow-palmed folk can have a cruel streak and find it hard to socialize, especially in groups.

However, you must take account of the fact that if you are studying the hand of a slim, short person, this type of palm will be completely normal for them in a positive way.

Flexibility of the Hand

Flexible Hands

This person is restless and can soon lose interest in a project, sometimes not completing what they have started. They will need lots of stimulation, and when younger, can be a handful for their parents.

Inflexible Hands

These are sedentary types who love routine and prefer to stay at home in front of the television. Often they are unfeeling and cold with a rigid

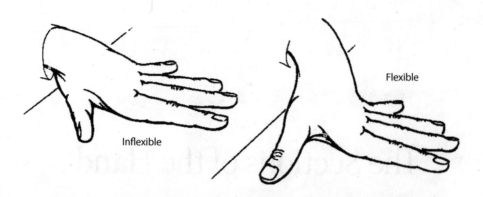

Inflexible

Flexible

outlook to life. They will isolate themselves and do anything for a quiet life.

Claw Shaped Hands

Claw shaped hands look like talons, and their owners tend to be greedy, with critical natures and sharp tongues. Often they are difficult to please; no matter how hard you try, they will never be satisfied and will make those close to them feel inadequate.

3

The Sections of the Hand

Auseful tip in palmistry is to look at the hand in three parts. It makes the synopsis easier and more accurate to predict. Palmists will take a print of the hand and then divide it into three sections to get a broader picture of their client.

Section One—The Perfect World

Section one shows the top of the fingers tapering down to the base of the fingers. This helps us to understand the person's hopes, dreams, and ambitions and how they view the world and their spiritual life.

Well-Formed Fingers

If the fingers (especially the Saturn finger) are well formed, it shows the person is well balanced. Taking a tape measure, find out if this is the longest section of the hand; if it is, your subject will enjoy academic study and will have a thirst for learning. He will literally be a walking encyclopedia and a wonderful teacher. If this part of the hand is shorter, then the opposite applies.

Section Two—The Practical World

This is the middle section of the hand and reveals a wealth of knowledge. It runs from the base of the fingers and encompasses both lower and higher Mars Mounts and the Quadrangle.

Wide Space

When this is the deepest and widest part of the palm, we have an owner who will be very practical and able to put his hand to most things. These

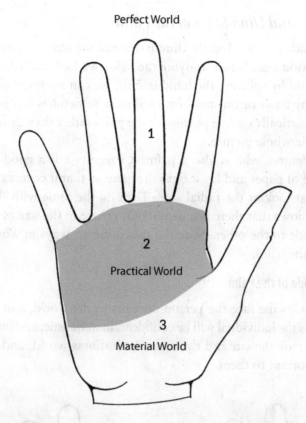

Perfect World

1

2

Practical World

3

Material World

people will usually have their own business, which will run like clockwork. They can be quite inventive, especially if they are in the building trade, and they can be a Jack-of-all-trades. These folk are the salt of the earth. They are efficient and good timekeepers.

Section Three—The Material World

This formation runs from the bottom of the Mars mounts and encompasses the mount of Venus, the Neptune mount, and the rascettes.

If this is the more pronounced area of the hand, these people will want financial security above everything else. They consider their own desires and needs, and while they can talk the talk and walk the walk, when it boils down to it, they put themselves first every time. If the space is balanced and not too heavy, the individual will enjoy cash but not allow it to rule them, and they will be hard working, tenacious, and kind.

The Radial and Ulna Sides of the Palm

The radial side is located on the thumb side and the ulna is on the opposite, percussion side. When studying the palm, we look for balance and harmony, and by splitting the hand in half, we can see more clearly if there are any flaws or outstanding attributes. Sometimes it is better to work systematically on one portion of the palm rather than drifting the eyes over the whole picture.

Sasha Fenton, who is also a palmist, suggests it is a good idea to take a piece of paper and lay it onto the hand so that it covers the ulna side and just look at the radial side. Then do the same with the ulna side. This shows that there is a distinct difference in the size of a hand from one side to the other. Note the two different ways in which you can divide the hand.

The Radial Side of the Palm

This represents the face the person presents to the world, and a good radial shows the individual will be confident, materialistic, and outgoing. They will enjoy the cut and thrust of the business world, and money will be important to them.

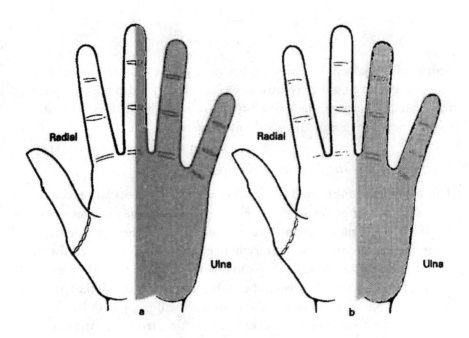

A Pronounced Radial

Those who have pronounced radials are ambitious and energetic; the world is their oyster and they strive to do well at everything. These people are competitive and materialistic. Their lack of spiritual belief can make them seem rather shallow. Their sex drive will be high, but they will lack the tenderness of a true lover and will soon move on to the next challenge, as they love variety. These people are assertive in business and although ruthless, can be fair and generous bosses.

A Pronounced Ulna

People with this formation are vulnerable and emotional. They yearn to paint, draw, and write, but their lack of confidence will hold them back, so their efforts usually result in failure. They are indecisive and will often let others make decisions for them, becoming resentful and dissatisfied with their lives when it doesn't work out. It is quite rare to see a pronounced ulna however, because the majority of people have a more balanced hand.

Equal Balance

When both sides of the palm are equally balanced, the owners will be fairly easy going and will enjoy life to the fullest. They are kind, have a good sense of humor, and can see the bigger picture in life. Because they have many talents, from the scientific to the creative, and lead a happy family life, they enjoy their lives to the fullest.

The Percussion Edge of the Hand

The percussion section of the hand tells us a lot about the nature and character of the person and also the places they might visit in the world. Health issues can sometime show up here, too. The following diagrams will help you to ascertain the different types you might encounter.

Flat Percussion (b)

If the side of the percussion appears flat and thin on its outline, the owner of this hand will often have no stamina or staying power. Perhaps their energy levels will come in fits and starts, and they need to have plenty of rest and pauses to recharge their batteries. Sometimes their libido is quite low.

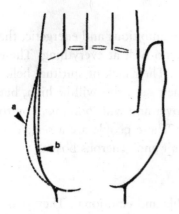

Low Bulbous Percussion

The lower percussion will be quite dominant in sporty types. The owners of this type of hand will be outgoing, living on their adrenalin, enjoying sports and outdoor pursuits. Their libido will be high and they can be quite promiscuous until they find their true love. As they are restless, they must have plenty of variety in their lives. Often they will take jobs that involve travel or exploration, and they like to get off the beaten track. Others could successfully choose acting or dancing as a career.

The Middle Bulbous Percussion (a)

These subjects are attractive, amusing, intuitive and highly creative, and they can captivate an audience with their fascinating personality. This is a psychic hand, and those who are not sure of their gift or who are in denial of this gift, might have to be encouraged to pay attention to their dream sleep and to record their dreams. It would also be a good idea for them to attend meditation and self-awareness groups. On the whole, they should already be on their path and will often be clairvoyant and into esoteric and holistic pursuits.

Rounded Percussion

These folk live on their nerves and are very highly strung, fidgety, and restless. They can lack concentration. Often they will miss out on today because they will be worrying about tomorrow. As a whole, they will benefit from such things as meditation, yoga, or an aromatherapy session.

Full Percussion

Whenever you see a full percussion, the owners of this hand will be highly imaginative and sensitive, with scant regard for material possessions. They make good writers, especially if there is a trident on the end of the head line.

Boxed Percussion

This is similar to the square shaped hand, so these folks thrive on hard work and outdoor activities. They will sometimes neglect relationships because they will often be workaholics. On the plus side, they are great fun to be with, but can be a little staid in the bedroom.

Thick and Thin Percussions

Those with thick percussions can cope with a lot of stress, as nothing seems to faze them. If the edge is thin, then the opposite applies. The owners can be sensitive, easily hurt, and upset.

part two

HAND
TOPOGRAPHY

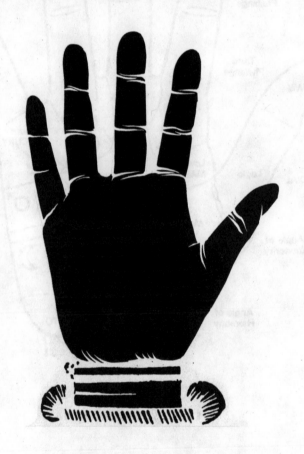

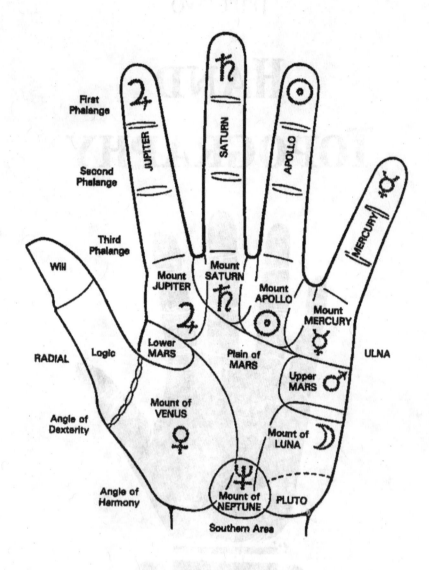

THE LANDSCAPE OF THE HAND

4

The Knuckles

Ask your client to make a fist without gripping too hard, and then ask them to hold their arms down so that you can see the knuckles clearly. Look at the back of the hand to see if one knuckle stands out as being larger than the rest. When a person gets older, the knuckles can sometimes swell with arthritis or rheumatism, so that must be taken into consideration when reading the hand.

Larger Jupiter Knuckle

As this finger represents a subject's image, self-confidence, and ego, large Jupiter knuckles show good self-esteem, and individuals would do well if self-employed. When over-large, these types can be prone to arrogance.

Small Jupiter Knuckle

These owners will lack confidence and be easily led. They dislike having to think for themselves and hang back in the workplace, refusing to take responsibility.

Large Saturn Knuckle

The Saturn finger represents everyday life, our responsibilities, and also our consciousness. Those who have large Saturn knuckles are responsible types and think hard about their day-to-day activities. If they say they will do something, they do it rather than let others down. These individuals are good leaders and fair bosses, which makes them popular. Over-large knuckles belong to folk who are inclined to restrict themselves by conforming to rigid rules.

Small Saturn Knuckle

These types care little for others and will always look for the easy way out. They hate responsibility and will take a long time to grow up. Because of their immaturity, their relationships can be a nightmare.

Large Apollo Knuckle

This is the finger of optimism and creativity. When the Apollo knuckles are the largest on the hand, it signifies those who are captivated by art of any sort. They love to work in areas of creativity, they will have a good eye for fashion and interior design, and they may sit for hours using their skills with cake crafting, card making and sewing. If the knuckle is very dominant, there will be a wonderful flair present and the owner might find media fame.

Small Apollo Knuckle

There will be little interest in art or craft, although they will love to visit galleries and might well have an interest in fashion. They will, however, lack the creative skills to develop their own style.

Large Mercury Knuckle

Mercury represents oration, communication, and truth. A large Mercury knuckle is indicative of the gift for speech or perhaps a lovely singing voice, which can captivate others. Its owner hates to tell lies and will be a seeker of truth. As they enjoy company, they will feel at home in a group or large family setting. If the knuckle is over-large, the person will star in some sort of television or media work.

Small Mercury Knuckle

This person could be shy and a little tongue-tied. They love to mix with others, but stay in the background rather than get too involved. Sometimes they will have trouble expressing themselves artistically, and they constantly put themselves down.

Smooth Knuckles

When all of the knuckles are smooth and of the same proportions, the owner will be psychic, impulsive, and day-dreamy.

Knotted Knuckles

Those who have knuckles that are knotted and deeply grooved are inclined to have tunnel vision and don't like to be told anything. They tend to be know-alls who may enjoy forcing their opinions on others.

Under Developed Knuckles

Low self-esteem comes with this formation, and the owner will have a painfully shy nature. They will be kind and generous, and, as my grandmother would say, "the better for knowing." Sometimes they suffer a little with their health as they have a delicate constitution.

Full Range

When the knuckles are a full range with plenty of peaks and valleys, the person will enjoy good health and stamina.

5

The Mounts

Holding your hand in front of you, look down across the palm to see the mounts. Larger mounts signify more vitality, caused by brain energy flowing into them. Consider the mounts as hills, the Plain of Mars the valley and the lines as rivers and inlets.

THE VENUS MOUNT

This mount is set on the fleshy part of the thumb and it is the largest mount on the hand. It represents love, passion, libido, and emotion. The family and friendship areas are to be found here too, as are gifts in the social arts.

Large, red Venus mounts belong to those who are over-fond of food and alcohol, and who like their creature comforts. They can be

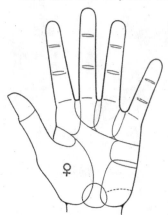

obsessive about sex and will seek new ways to keep their libido energized. These types are sometimes referred to as "body people."

Medium Venus mounts represent a good balance. These types enjoy the finer aspects of life, as well as enjoying a happy and contented home life where they will make steady and caring parents.

Those with a flat or hard Venus mount have quite cold natures and can be difficult to get to know, as their characters are rather shallow. They don't always enjoy good health, have a lack of resistance to germs, and sometimes have a poor appetite. My grandmother, who taught me old fashioned palmistry, used to say these individuals are prone to being frigid. Narrow and flat mount types are sometimes called "mind people." A narrow Mount of Venus doesn't denote a lack of interest in sex, although it does indicate an inability to give and receive love easily. A cramped and flat Venus shows an active mind and a person who will fantasize about sex rather than enact it.

In short, the bon-vivant has the large Venus mount while the esthete has the smaller one.

THE JUPITER MOUNT

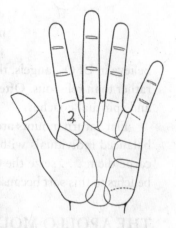

The Jupiter mount sits at the base of the index or Jupiter finger and when over-large, these folk are inclined to expend too much energy on projects that won't get finished. Gambling might be an interest, and they take chances for the sheer hell of it. As they have a taste for the good things in life and a great deal of vanity, their lives can be like a tangled ball of string.

Those who have medium-sized Jupiter mounts are enterprising and become good leaders. They have an ambitious streak. As bosses, they will be fair and like to bring out the best in their staff. They hate bullies. As they have a thirst for knowledge and an interest in languages, they will often study and take exams, even into old age.

When the Jupiter mount is flat, the owner can have low self-esteem and seek out friends who are happy to tell them what to do. They will cling to the family unit and will need others to make decisions for them. Because they take a long time to grow up, they will often lack skills in practical things and have low standards. Many are clumsy, untidy, and forgetful.

THE SATURN MOUNT

The Saturn mount sits at the base of the middle finger, and it is often a flat area or even a valley rather than an actual mount. However, hands vary tremendously, so actual mounts do appear here on occasion. In old-fashioned palmistry, this was classed as the health mount, which is

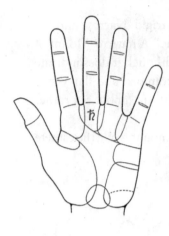

associated with the bones, teeth, spleen, and gall bladder. In some ways, I feel it is better not to have too strong a Saturn mount.

Over-large Saturn mounts suggest pessimism and sombre, doom and-gloom types. When in the company of these people, others feel they have to cheer them up, as they tend to be such wet blankets. These people can sometimes have an interest in the black arts.

Medium-sized Saturn mounts denote those who are constructive. These subjects enjoy meditation, getting messages during dream-sleep, and receiving prophesies. They may believe in UFOs, angels, the spirit world and anything that is New Age rather than religious. Often they will work as healers, aromatherapists, and spiritual coaches.

Flat Saturn mounts are better than raised ones as they indicate well-balanced individuals with a wide outlook on life. Their motto will be carpe diem . . . seize the day! An optimistic nature will usually bring benefits to this sort because what they send out, they get back three-fold.

THE APOLLO MOUNT

Some palmists call this the Mount of the Sun. Either way, it's the mount under the ring or Apollo finger. I class it as a happy mount, as there are so many good things that surround it.

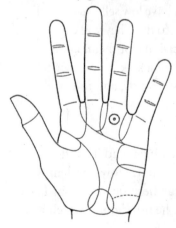

Large Apollo mounts represent people who are talented, inspired, and probably connected with the media or fame. They will shine in anything they pursue, which might be dance, art, music, and writing, while fate will give them lashings of help along the way. Also, with this formation, the owner will love children and parenting.

Medium Apollo mount owners have magnetism, flair, and a sense of fun. They will lighten a party, bring laughter, and will have original ideas.

When the Apollo mount is flat, the owner will lack social graces and can be somewhat gauche. As if to compensate for their lack of talent, they will have a misguided sense of their own importance. These are the kinds of people we see on talent shows who are puffed up and full of self-esteem, only to be knocked down and brought into the real world. Their worst faults are being pompous and attention seeking.

THE MERCURY MOUNT

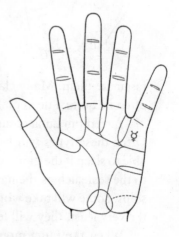

The Mercury mount is found at the base of the little finger and it leans toward the percussion side of the hand. The Mercury mount represents intellect, brainpower, and a thirst for knowledge.

People who have large Mercury mounts have, so to speak, large brain-boxes. Ask them a question and you have your own personal encyclopedia. They will know exactly where Macchu Picchu is on the map, and they may even have been there, because they love to travel. They have an appetite for science and will often make wonderful teachers. They are quick witted, funny, and good communicators.

When the Mercury mount is medium in size the owners will take an interest in their health and make sure they get plenty of fresh air and vitamins. You can't fool them, because they are very shrewd and can see through you and spot your problems and faults in an instant. If the Mercury finger is pointed with a medium mount, we have psychic powers present in the owner.

A low Mercury mount is often found on the hands of those who, as children, had difficulties when learning to read or write and were slower at school than their peer group. They will be a little clumsy and prone to silly accidents and forgetfulness. Their nature will still be positive, but the nervous system will often let them down.

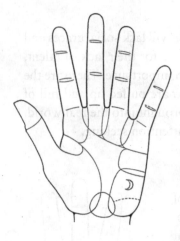

THE LUNA MOUNT

This is also known as the Moon Mount and it is located on the lower percussion, just above the wrist. As the moon is very mysterious, so is this mount. The old-fashioned palmists, like gypsies, would study this in great detail.

A large Luna mount represents an interest in all things mystic and psychic, such as tarot cards, runes, and divination, while trance work connected to mediumship will fascinate them. Many clairvoyants have a raised Luna mount that can often be quite a deep pink color.

A medium Luna mount owner will love water and especially the sea. Often these types will be affected by the moon cycles and will not be able to sleep if the moon is new or full. They tend to seek jobs connected to the sea, such as the navy, the merchant navy, and working on cruise ships. Some will take work as fisherman, divers, and oil-rig workers. At the very least, they will love to travel.

When the Luna mount is flat, the person will have little intuition and a more practical nature, preferring to stick to well-known methods. If at all religious, they will keep to the strict teachings of the church. They will, however, have a protective instinct for their loved ones and will love animals.

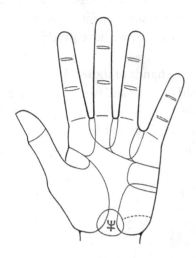

THE NEPTUNE MOUNT

A large Neptune mount is quite rare. It is placed just above the wrist and is small and round, like a button.

A large Neptune mount will give protection on the water, so palmists like to see this with fishermen and navy personnel. Owners of a large mount will seek holistic and esoteric knowledge and could have jobs in homeopathic practices, reflexology, shiatsu, aromatherapy, and hypnosis.

A medium Neptune mount belongs on the hands of those who come into such things later on in their lives, perhaps after having a more conventional job. They will soon catch up and might practice the healing arts right up until old age.

When the Neptune Mount is flat, this would be classed as quite normal. It does not portray anything bad, just a normal attitude to mainstream life.

THE MARS MOUNT

The Lower Mount of Mars

This mount sits in toward the percussion side of the hand, below the head line and in the Quadrangle. It is associated with resistance.

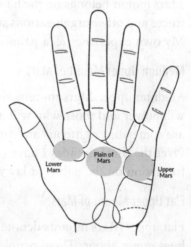

Large Lower Mount of Mars

Those who have a large lower Mars mount are courageous and may choose to work in the police force, the fire service, as paramedics, or in the armed services. Females have tenacity and strength, sometimes out performing a man.

Medium Lower Mount of Mars

Medium lower Mars mounts predict a rational view of life, someone who can do things on the spur of the moment and whose ideas often turn out well. They have lively personalities and will always stay motivated. We often find this type of person will gravitate toward self-employment.

Flat Lower Mount of Mars

Flat lower Mars mounts people show a lack of energy, are not aggressive, and can often end up being bullied or put upon. Health wise, there might be conditions with the blood, adrenal glands, and kidneys.

Upper Mount of Mars

This mount sits in between the forefinger and the thumb.

Large Upper Mount of Mars

A large upper Mars mount shows good recovery from illness and great stamina. These individuals don't like being inactive; they enjoy getting on with life. They don't sit still for more than five minutes, so they can be restless and bad tempered if illness keeps them tethered.

According to the well-known palmist Malcolm Wright, a large upper Mars mount belongs on the hands of those who like being in the armed forces and other organizations such as the scouts, guides, and sea cadets. My own experience as a palmist has borne this out.

Medium Upper Mount of Mars

Medium upper Mars mounts show up on those who have stamina and will power and those who will not often stray off the beaten path. They are somewhat righteous and single-minded but will have good hearts. Over the three decades I have been a palmist, I have often noticed this formation on the palms of lawyers, magistrates, and prison officers.

Flat Upper Mount of Mars

Flat upper Mars mounts denote low stamina and little resistance to any bugs going about. These people will take time to heal and need plenty of sleep.

The Plain of Mars

The Plain of Mars (shown in the illustration on page 33), sits in the central part of the palm and tells us a lot about the personality of the seekers, also about their trials and tribulations. Most of the major lines of the hand pass through this triangular space, so ancient Vedic palmists would spend hours studying this area to gain maximum information.

When this area is crossed with fragmented lines, crosses, grilles and squares, the owners will face huge obstacles in their lives. Many of these problems will be caused by their own lack of judgment and immaturity, which in turn will make life difficult for their families and partners. I have found in my experience as a palmist that these types are not good at managing money and seldom hold down a job for long. They may rely on others to get them out of trouble and will often sponge off friends and family. If the Plain of Mars is blemish-free, then the subjects will be level headed, healthy, and will put their backs into life.

The Pond

If the central palm is hollow, this is referred to as "the pond." Often when this formation is present, the owners will be low on energy, not sleeping well, or recovering from an illness. When health is restored, the pond will often plump up to show that their vitality has returned.

Triangular Plain of Mars

When there is an obvious triangular shape in the Plain of Mars, these individuals are suffering from suppressed anger and resentment. Their moods will be unpredictable and they can suddenly lash out. This area will be red, blotchy, and slightly damp. These types have many hang-ups and insecurities and some may have a slightly perverted nature.

A Bony Plain of Mars

When the Plain of Mars is wafer thin and under-developed, these people will lack confidence in their outward appearance and their inner talents and abilities. Sometimes these characters can be very good actors, hiding an inner shyness while presenting a brave face to the world.

Over-Developed Plain of Mars

This will sit quite high up in the palm, and its texture can be hard and fleshy. The owners will be thick skinned and lacking in manners. They don't listen to good advice and will have to learn by their mistakes. In Vedic palmistry, this character would be classed as "a young soul" who has much to learn.

part three

THE LINES OF
THE HAND

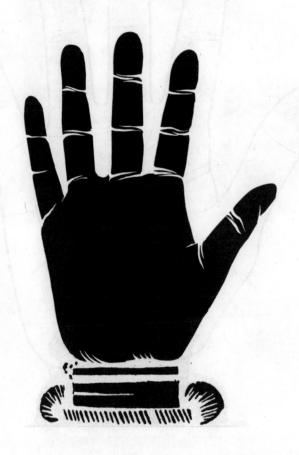

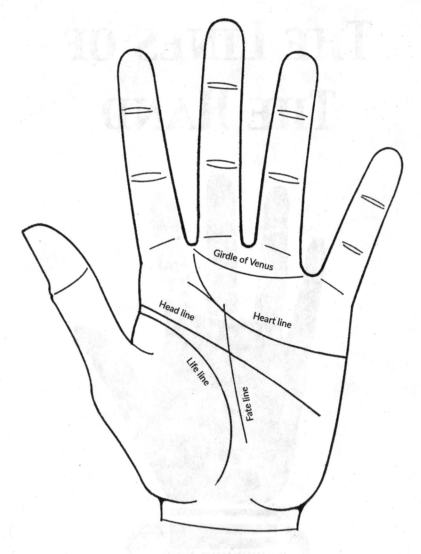

Girdle of Venus

Head line

Heart line

Life line

Fate line

THE MAJOR LINES

6

Major Lines

The "major" lines of the hand are the Life Line, the Head Line, the Heart Line, and the Fate Line. You have no doubt heard of these lines; they are the ones that most readily come to mind when one thinks of "reading the palm." In this chapter we will also discuss Simian Lines and the Girdle of Venus, since they are both related to the major lines.

THE LIFE LINE

The life line is the most vital line on the hand and holds huge importance to palmists. It starts between the Jupiter finger and thumb, and circles around the fleshy part of the Mount of Venus, often heading down toward the rascettes of Venus for its termination point. Older palmistry traditions tell us that the life line can reveal the length of life. It certainly reveals the condition of our health, including such things as accidents and our management of health problems. Travel can also be seen on this line.

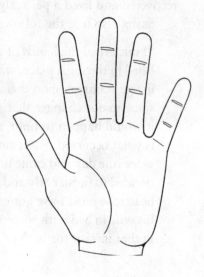

A Short or Broken Life line

A short life line often depicts a major change of life at some point, after which the individual's life will be very different. Frequently, after the

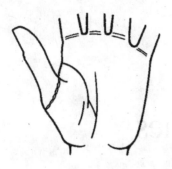

line stops, its energies are transferred to an extra line, which may be a recycled and reversed part of the fate line. I say recycled and reversed, because the fate line normally rises up the hand toward the fingers, but when the lower part takes over the job of the life line, you have to read that section of it downward.

Sometimes the life line is weak, broken, or even missing in parts, but the head line strengthens by way of compensation, and takes over some of the work of the life line.

While on the subject of strange life lines, Sasha remembers one lady who had no life line at all on her non-dominant hand, and asked her if anything life-threatening had happened to her. This lady told her that she had been in a terrible accident at the age of four and had not been expected to live, but modem medicine had done its magic and she recovered and lived a perfectly normal life thereafter.

Sasha also tells the following story:

"I once read the hands of a married couple whose life lines finished in the same place, with the classical 'move to the fate line' image stamped upon them. I told them they could both expect some major changes that would be sudden and dramatic, and it would happen to both of them at about the same time. This is what occurred. Some time after the reading, the chap was at work one day and came down with a migraine headache, so he decided to finish early and go home. When he arrived home, his headache must have gotten much worse because he discovered his wife in bed with someone else! Needless to say, life changed in that instant for both of them!"

Key Points

Try not to predict the exact length of someone's life, even if all the indications on the hand suggest a short life span. Also take into consideration that the left hand is what is given and the right hand is what you do with it. If a person is left handed, then this process is reversed.

My mother, Betty, had quite a long life line on her left hand, going somewhere toward the mid-eighties, but her right hand told a very different story, as it predicted that she would not live to see old age. She had been a heavy smoker since being a teenager, and this caught up with her, so that she died at the age of fifty-nine from lung cancer. I have often given stern warnings when reading for smokers, and I'm inclined not to hold back, especially if there is a narrowing in the central quadrangle, which can predict emphysema or asthmatic problems. On the brighter side, I have also saved lives with these warnings.

Can a Short Life Line Grow as We Get Older?

Yes it can. My husband, John, had a very short but vital life line and judging by the time scale on his hand, according to old palmistry traditions, he should have gone to meet his maker at about thirty-five years of age. Over the years, his life line has steadily grown and has become quite strong. Vedic palmists believe if you are sad or unsettled, the life line can be short and thin, but when there is a purpose and thirst for life, the life line becomes stronger and longer.

Does a Break in the Life Line Mean the End?

No it doesn't. A break in a life line can mean, "off with the old and on with the new." If there is no cross on either broken line, then it bodes well. If a cross is present, then there might be an accident or sudden setback for the individual. If a square sits around the cross, then protection will be given.

Long, Clear Life Lines

This can mean good health and sturdy vitality, and such people bounce back from illness quickly. They will happily meet the challenges that come their way and will have lots of energy, even when they go into old age.

Sexy Life Lines

If the life line is especially red, then a passionate nature will be present and the individual will have a healthy libido.

Sick Life Lines

Sometimes you can see the life line is lackluster and very thin and fragmented, especially if the hand has a satiny shine to it; this means fatigue and sickness. Tassels will be present, or chains and grilles cutting across the life line, giving it an untidy appearance and a lack of conformity.

High Life Lines

These start quite high on the mount of Jupiter and show a driven nature that will do anything to succeed. These types will be highly ambitious and enjoy the cut and thrust of competition and business. They will have many irons in the fire and will have a thirst for intellectual interests. They will often further their education when older, going on to get a degree later in life.

Low Life Lines

A life line that starts just above the thumb suggests a personality that is uncomplicated and without ambition. The owners will prefer to live a simple life with their creature comforts and small circle of friends and family around them. They will have plenty of energy though, and will be on the go most of the time, but won't like to dwell too much on intellectual pursuits.

Common Life Lines

When the line starts between the Jupiter finger and the thumb there is a well-balanced aspect. These people will be eager to pursue life with a good degree of common sense and optimism. They will not want to be the best or the worst at anything, and such subjects will be ready for what fate offers. These people make laid-back parents who encourage their offspring in all things pertaining to education and hobbies.

THE HEAD LINE

The head line tells us how an individual thinks, and it shows their mental ability. It also tells a great deal about the path of their career, finances, hobbies, interests, and the way these people use their mental faculties.

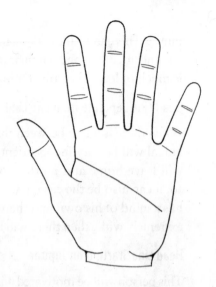

Head Line Linked to the Life Line

The head and life lines often grow out of one line (a), and as long as they part fairly quickly on the hand, this is no bad thing. These people have a strong sense of family duty, and they may not be in a hurry to leave home and become independent.

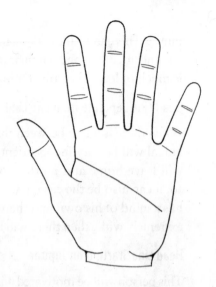

Head line variations

Head Line Tied to the Life Line

When these two lines are tied for a long stretch at the start, the owners have a strong sense of family duty and may also lack the courage to stride out on their own. They cling to the clan for support and can be very selective about friendships. This situation isn't always due to a fear of leaving the nest, because there might be a reason for the ongoing family connection. For instance, there may be a handicapped or needy family member that the subject chooses to take care of, or at least be in regular contact with. Sometimes, an interfering parent wants to run the subject's life even after they are married with children of their own. In some cases, these people might marry and find themselves stuck with an unsavory partner, or dragged into a dreadful in-law situation where the spouse's parents, brothers, or sisters are utterly horrid and try to control them.

When this formation is present, another scenario can exist, where the subject can't make a decision without talking things over with the family. This can result in them handing over too much power to a parent, a family member, or even their partner. This is especially so if the partner is much older, richer, or of a higher class and has a controlling nature.

Head Line Separate from Life Line

When there is a gap between the head line and the life line (b), the individual will be very independent. Palmistry theory suggests these people will leave home and go their own way early in life; while this can be so, it can also be the case that the person stays near the family unit, but has a mind of his own and therefore sees no need to escape. If the gap is extremely wide, then there will be a tendency not to look before leaping.

Head Line Starting on Jupiter

This person will be motivated and a good organizer. With a driven nature, he will get much done and will be a good and fair boss.

Sloping Head Line

In Vedic palmistry, this represents those who are on a spiritual quest. They will seek out all things esoteric and try to improve their lives and the lives of others around them. If the head line sinks too low on the hand, they can have day-dreamy natures and won't have a grasp on reality.

Straight Head Line

These owners are realistic but somewhat blinded to any new ideas. They respect authority and like things done in a proper manner. In my experience, this type of person doesn't change his mind quickly and can be quite dogmatic.

Short Head Line

When the head line is short, these people don't strive too hard and can live mundane lives. They fear changes and challenges and prefer a regular routine to make them feel safe. As they are self-centered, they will talk endlessly about their hobbies, such as train spotting, golf, or gardening, and have no real interest in the conversation of others.

Their tempers are erratic and they are often unreasonable. If the line is red, they could have a violent streak and be prone to lash out in frustration. This is especially so if the line is short, straight, and then dips down suddenly at the end.

Long Head Line

The owner will be driven, energetic and have a great mental aptitude. Their memory will be second to none and they usually enjoy great success. The direction of the head line must be taken into account. If the line travels straight across the palm, there could be successes in math, science, and business, but if it slopes, the subject might enjoy art, writing, spirituality, creativity, and so on.

Break in Head Line

This person will have to take care of accidents, especially if the lines are overlapping. If a square is on the formation and connects the lines, then all will be well.

Bitty, Broken Head Line

Sometimes this can represent poor areas of concentration and the individual can be forgetful. If the head line has too many broken lines, large islands and grilles, the person could suffer with mental problems and erratic mood swings. Sometimes when studying the female hand, you will see these formations when they are hormonal. Further up the line it can become settled again when the problem has subsided. Check if the Luna mount is red or mottled to verify this.

Trident on the End of Head Line

When this is in place, the owner will be gifted with writing and there will be a strong probability of published work. If there is just an ordinary fork, then the gift of writing will still be there, but this time perhaps for the person's own pleasure or within an organization for commercial work, creating PowerPoint presentations and so on.

Chained Head Line

This can mean a predisposition toward cluster headaches for the individual, who could also be plagued with tiredness and apathy. When the chains are small and run along the whole of the head line, the owner could have eye problems. Their sight might be good one day but blurry the next. If this is an ongoing situation, recommend a visit to their doctor. If there is a largish island or a cluster of them below the area of the Saturn mount and finger, the person may suffer deafness, and if the same formation occurs below the Apollo mount and Apollo finger, there could be eye problems. If there are two large circles on the head line—and they have to be exactly round and red—then the person might suffer from glaucoma.

I remember reading the palm of a doctor many years ago and saw this formation on his hands. I asked if he had been suffering serious sight problems and then tentatively asked if he had seen an eye specialist. Bluntly, he asked, "What are you trying to say, Beleta?" Gently, I asked him if there was any glaucoma in his family. He replied abruptly "I had glaucoma diagnosed three months ago, is that what you are trying to tell me?"

This is a note from Sasha:

"Beleta amazed me when she came out with the comment about my fluctuating eyesight when she looked at my hands, because my sight does fluctuate. I have diabetes, and when there's too much sugar floating in my bloodstream, the lenses of one or both eyes become clouded. I sometimes suffer hemorrhages at the back of one or other of my eyes, which practically blinds me for a week or two at a time. Beleta told me that if the islands are pale, the eyesight will fluctuate, while if they are blue, red, or standing out in some other way, the problem is likely to be permanent."

Islands on the Head Line

Islands are slightly different from chains as they are longer and less rounded; often they will be called "slung loops chains" by a professional palmist. If they are seen on the palm, especially the head line, the owner will often feel trapped, perhaps in their marriage, relationship, or job.

If the rest of the hand is aggressive and angry, or when the person has the murderer's thumb, they might have done a spell in prison. If the islands are at the start of the head line, the person might have had an unhappy childhood in school or home life. See also the Cat's Cradle formation.

Cat's Cradle and Triangles

The cat's cradle looks like the children's game with string or wool. The children would make intricate patterns, which they entwined around their fingers. If this type of formation commences at the start of the head line and life line, it is often an indication that the person disliked school, or less commonly, the subject may have liked school, but used it as an escape from an unhappy home life. A sharp island that looks like a triangle hanging on the line can indicated the person wasn't free to follow their dreams. We rarely see this configuration now, but it was a common sight among young men who had done National Service and hated the experience. These days we might link it to someone who's done a short spell in prison or community service through criminal or antisocial behavior.

Twisted Wavy Head Line

These characters can be unstable and have a weak mentality. If they are addicted to drink or drugs, they can be unpredictable. They could even be bipolar.

Arched Head Line

These are tough, determined individuals who set out to get what they want and can be ruthless. Unconcerned about the feelings of others, they can crush anyone who gets in their way.

Upward Branches

These types listen to their heads rather than their hearts, and they are usually very successful in all they do because of their focused nature. If the branches drop down, then there could be a period of bad luck for the individual.

Crosses

Not a good omen, as the owners will be prone to bad luck and upsets throughout their lives. These folk need to take great care to do everything properly as they can soon find themselves in a muddle through lack of forethought.

Purple Dots

If purple dots are present, the owner has to take great care of head injuries. If a square surrounds the dot, then protection will be given.

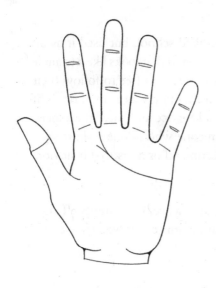

THE HEART LINE

There can be controversy about where the heart line begins. Some traditional palmists say that it begins under the Mercury mount while the Vedic palmists say it begins under the Jupiter mount, and as this is a book that inclines toward Vedic palmistry, we will take the latter pathway.

The heart line can reveal much about the owner's emotional state and it can also offer information about health. Sometimes my clients are anxious because their heart line is broken and short. Younger people think their marriages will be short-lived or unhappy when this is present on their hands, so when this happens I reassure them that there are many things on the palm that concern love and relationships and that one line cannot be taken in isolation, as it won't show the full picture.

Trident Fork at the Source on the Jupiter Mount

This is a really lovely thing to see as it represents a spiritual person who will help many in their lifetime due to their wonderful insight and inspiration. In Vedic palmistry, this mark can represent an "earth avatar type" who has come to earth to change the way people think. My grandmother linked this formation to clairvoyance and dream sleep premonitions.

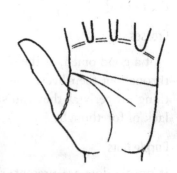

Long straight heart line

Long Straight Heart Line

These individuals are loyal, loving, and caring to their partners, families, and friends, especially if the heart line is unbroken. The line should have a nice rosy tinge of pink.

Short Heart Line

I have found that short heart lines belong to very down-to-earth individual's of both sexes who can be single minded in their pursuit of love. If the heart line blends with the attachment lines, the person will want to have the upper hand in relationships and family matters. They can often be insecure and make themselves unpopular because of their outdated Victorian principles. We see this type of heart line more often now, as many couples enter mixed marriages, so there can be issues if men from Eastern religions marry Western women who are used to a more independent lifestyle.

Weak and Fragmented Heart Line

One interpretation for this line is that these people can be unfaithful and inconsistent in love or friendships. As they are prone to change their minds, being in a relationship with them can be a bit of a roller-coaster ride. Where marriages are concerned, they are usually doomed to failure. They may fall in love with people who are engaged or married to someone else. They could also go for the types that are into drugs or drink and crime. I often call them "the victims." I have found they rarely value their friends, and pick them up and put them down at will. These individuals will drone on for hours about their problems, but will not be interested if their friends need a shoulder to cry on. As they set themselves up for failure before they start, friends and family will often have to bail them out and wait for them to grow up.

Islands on the Heart Line

The owner will be prone to deceit or affairs and can cause heartache within relationships. This can happen in reverse, where the subject is decent but their partner is not. Sasha and I agree with our friend Malcolm Wright, who says he has often found that an isolated island shows that a relationship has come to a sudden end, for example, a partner going out for a pint of milk and never returning. If the island is under the Apollo finger, there could be eye problems for the person.

Broken Heart Line

A break in an otherwise decent looking heart line can signify a broken heart. If the line starts up again and becomes strong, these subjects don't ever forget what has happened to them, but they do move on to live, love, and be happy again.

Squares on the Heart Line

This can represent extreme tension for the individual, and they could suffer from their nerves. As squares represent protection, they usually weather the storm and come out smiling. Another common scenario is that the person's emotional life is temporarily restricted. This can be because they feel alone, or they may be longing for love because they are in an unloving relationship.

Downward Branches

If there are quite a few of these, a series of disappointments and quarrels could occur for the person. These, however, are usually short-lived.

Upward Branches

This is a good thing to see on the heart line as it represents success, love, and new friendships that could be long lasting.

Circles on the Heart Line

This can mean the owner will have to take care with problems of the heart. If they are overweight this could be a serious matter. As I said earlier in the book, a palmist is not here to diagnose or frighten their clients, so caution is warranted when giving a reading.

Wavy Heart Line

This too can sometimes mean cardiac trouble or problems with the blood. It can also denote uncertainty with the person's focus in life.

Double Heart Line

This looks as though the subject has two heart lines. The second heart line can repair any defects of the original heart line, especially if the original is untidy and small. Its owner will be very devoted with old-fashioned principles.

Heart Line Running Right Across the Hand

This line will be very long and not often seen. It represents a person who is acutely sensitive and aware of everything that is going on in their environment. They will have high empathy with animals, world issues, and mankind. Often life will make them feel depressed or hopeless because of their respect for the condition of all living things.

The Twig

When a short line sits horizontally on top of the heart line on the Saturn mount, this can represent divorce or separation. If there is another line on top of that, there could be more than one divorce for the person. If seen on a younger client's hand, be sure to tell them, "marry in haste, you'll repent at leisure." It would be better for them to wait for marriage until they reach the late twenties or early thirties to be sure of real happiness in love.

THE SIMIAN LINE

The Simian line (also known as the Single Transverse Palmar Crease) is formed when the head and heart lines fuse together into one crease, and it commences between the Jupiter finger and the thumb. Emotional and mental energies blend together to give the owner a struggle between thoughts and emotion. If seen on both hands, which can be quite rare, the owner could be highly creative, inventive, and unique, especially with art or writing. If the line is present only on the nondominant hand, its owner can have an erratic energy that could cause mayhem within their lives. If seen on only the dominant hand, the person could have an effect on others, perhaps in a disturbing or cathartic way. One thing for sure is that the lessons learned will help the soul to grow to a better understanding and awaken it to a deeper spiritual consciousness.

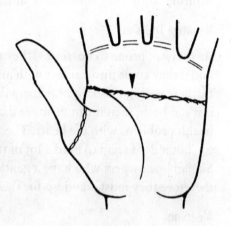

The name Simian comes from the word monkey or ape, because old time palmists assumed that it was seen on some primates' palms.

There is much controversy and research on the Simian line, which causes huge differences of opinion in the world of palmistry. Some say there is a higher percentage of the Simian line formation seen in Down syndrome people or babies with prenatal rubella and leukemia, and a host of other health problems have been mentioned in different books and articles. Others will argue that the Simian line is more abundant in certain cultures. There seems to be an agreement that there is a bigger percentage of this line in ethnic groups, and that it is more often seen in the male hand than the female.

Often a client will be horrified to be told they have this line and imagine all sorts of disturbing things, so reassurances have to be given and the bigger picture explained clearly to them. In modern day palmistry, we are inclined to be less critical of this formation. A Simian line owner can be highly intellectual, hold down a powerful job, and inspire others with their determination and tenacity. A prime example is ex-Prime Minister Tony Blair, who has a Simian line on each hand.

Negative Traits

As they are prone to bossiness, they must take care not to upset others, and if they come into contact with another bossy person, then often the feathers will fly! Usually the line will be present only in one hand, but if it's in both, then it can be more dramatic, and palmistry can point to health problems with the heart. There is not much research to back this up, but it does seem to hold a lot of truth in my experience as a palmist. Simian line owners who have a gentle nature can sometimes be bullied, therefore they must stand up for their beliefs.

Meaning

A Simian line owner will be intense and highly focused, to the point of obsession; their drive and ambition will be second to none and they can achieve great things. Their personality is tense and hyperactive and they can be totally consumed with themselves, overriding others who stand in their way. They will find it hard to separate emotions from thoughts and will hold deep secrets in their hearts. Many will be interested in religion. Others will want to deviate to a more liberal spiritual belief, but even so, they will still live by tradition. When they are in power, their unwavering focus can get much done, but because they can be so rigid, they are likely to upset others, and this can bring negativity in its wake. On a plus point, they have a wicked sense of humor and can be great fun to be with; when times are good they become excited, happy, and joyful.

In Love

Simian line owners are said to be secretive about their love life and don't often reveal their feelings for someone until they are very sure. As they don't like to be manipulated, they can often go for a weaker type of partner whom they can influence. In the bedroom, there can still be some control, but once they are truly in love, the barriers should come down.

Their only fault is that they could neglect their loved ones for work, as their burning ambition will take precedence.

As a parent, they can be exacting and want the best for their children. They won't be a pushover either, as they will have strong principles and traditional ideas of discipline. Many parents are softened by their love for their children and will bend the rules for them, but a Simian line type can be less sentimental.

Semi-Simian Line

This formation has a very short, stick-like heart line. These owners do not blend well in society and are difficult to talk to, as they are neurotic and obsessive. Through recent years, I have seen more autistic or mentally challenged youngsters with this configuration. Often they will be obsessed with video and computer games and take a long time to reach maturity. Sadly, this type will rarely be happy in love and can end up repressed and lonely.

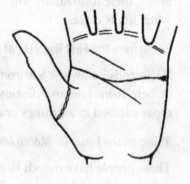

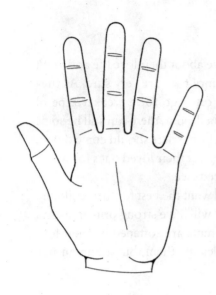

THE FATE LINE

This important line has a wealth of information for the seeker. It will reveal a person's destiny, fortune, and career, not to mention character. Some palmists, who also happen to be into astrology, link this line with Saturn. It often travels up the hand toward the Mount of Saturn, although it can go in a variety of directions.

Rising from the Neptune Mount

When the fate line starts from the Neptune mount and ascends to the Saturn finger, these individuals will likely have a long life and a natural ending when life is done.

Rising from the First Rascette of Venus

If this ends below the Saturn finger then it portrays a good life with lots of help from fate and destiny to help the owners on their way. These types succeed in all things and make a mark on the world.

Rising on the Lunar (or Moon) Mount

These people have moods that are very much affected by the moon and they have a psychic nature. Their lives are ruled by fate, which makes them winners at times, but they become badly blocked when they try to change their destiny in any way. This position is often found on the hands of white witches or people who follow the Wiccan belief. In Vedic palmistry this represents an old soul who has reincarnated to help others. Those who have fate lines that start on Luna will be valued by people far and wide, but not necessarily appreciated or understood within their own family.

Rising from the Life Line

When the fate line rises from the life line, the person will have to strive for their happiness and create their own success. As they don't always believe in destiny giving them a hand, they will work hard, and they will be envied and admired by those around them. If the line starts from the Mount of Venus, inside the life line, they may work in a family business, inherit money that will give them a good start in life, or have a very supportive and loving family around them.

A Long, Strong Fate Line

Fate plays a big part in these people's lives, which will be eventful, especially if the line has a lot of disturbance on it. A very long line with little disturbance is found on the hands of those who find their way early in life and see things through with little change. They may also have a keen work ethic and a strong sense of duty.

Starting Late on the Hand

Many individuals have fate lines that don't start until half way up the palm or even higher. These types may drift along until fate throws something at them and then, belatedly, they make an effort in life.

Termination on the Mount of Jupiter

This is a sign of success, but it can be at the cost of the individuals' personal lives, possibly because they put more energy into their careers than into loving relationships.

Termination on the Mount of Saturn

If the line is neat and not tasselled, the owners will be well prepared for life and will be successful after a period of hard work.

Termination on the Head Line

This isn't a good sign, as these people are prone to being slapdash. They don't think ahead and so make many mistakes that others will have to rectify. I find this type take a long time to grow up and they blame others for their misfortunes. In Vedic palmistry, such a person would be regarded as a young soul who hasn't reincarnated very often and would need the support of their family to instruct them in life skills, sometimes even into their forties.

Horizontal Lines

If there are many horizontal lines clearly indicated on the fate line, it can be a difficult or disturbing life for the owner. They could be plagued with ill luck and unhappiness. In Vedic palmistry, this configuration can mean the owner is reincarnating to become a wiser soul by learning life's lessons the hard way.

Upward Branch

This is a fortunate line as it means the person will have a positive change. Their position will improve financially, and they could enjoy a more exciting life. If the line branches downward then the opposite could occur.

Triangle

When there is a triangle on the base of the fate line, this could mean some sort of scandal will hit the person's life and cause mayhem for the individual and their family.

Island

When an island is present on the fate line, there will be a period of hardship. It can even represent the loss of a spouse. If a square surrounds the island, the situation could be averted. If the line splits into a long island where two lines run parallel for a long way, the subject will suffer a sustained period of unhappiness. This can be self-induced. The main cause is they are hanging onto a situation or a person from their past.

One of Sasha's clients had a lengthy narrow island of this type and said her husband had left her, but it took her many years to come to terms with the fact. The poor woman had given up much of her life to longing, yearning, and fighting hard for something that was never going to happen. What a waste of a precious life!

GIRDLE OF VENUS

The Girdle of Venus is a semi circular line that sits high above the heart line and under the Apollo and Saturn fingers; it will be on or around the Apollo and Saturn mounts. Some people confuse this line with a double heart line so care must be taken to make the right diagnosis.

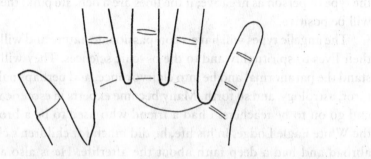

Not everyone has a Girdle of Venus, but many people have tasselled bits of one. New palmists sometimes link this line to sexuality and while it can relate somewhat to the libido, Vedic palmistry sees a strong Girdle of Venus as belonging to those who are driven and passionate about a project or particular aspect to their lives.

Traditional palmistry and Vedic palmistry disagree strongly with the formation of a perfectly formed Girdle of Venus. The traditional palmist sees a strong Girdle of Venus as a sign of weakness, signifying these subjects are emotionally destructive and can cause mayhem in their love lives. Traditionalists prefer to see a small and broken Girdle of Venus rather than a whole one, but Vedic palmistry takes the completely opposite view.

Fragmented Girdle of Venus

This person will not be as driven as those who have a complete Girdle of Venus, but they could have a talent for literary work. They are often inspired and highly sensitive and will love to mix with people who are like-minded. When I see this formation, which is rather like a wiry arc, I would encourage my client to join a writing circle.

Multiple Girdle of Venus

This formation has two or three (or more) strong, unbroken lines that sit directly under each other, and often the mounts will be red in color. There are two distinct types of person here; one could be called the angel and the other a devil. If the lines are very red, then I would class the type of person as negative; if the lines are a delicate pink, the person will be positive.

The angelic types will have a compassionate nature and will devote their lives to spirituality and to the psychic sciences. They will understand the paranormal and be into clairvoyance, and perhaps palmistry, tarot, astrology, and so forth. Many become experts in esoteric matters and go on to be teachers. I had a friend who used to be a brother of the White Eagle Lodge. In his life, he did much for children's charities abroad and had a deep faith about the afterlife. He is also a healer and a lover of the animal kingdom. The lines are very strong on his Girdle of Venus.

The diabolical type of person is preoccupied and obsessive about sex, and might have a stash of pornography to titillate the libido. These people may enhance their moods with stimulants, drugs, strip clubs, and prostitutes, and some will become obsessive about pornography websites.

Fragmented Multiples

If the double or triple lines on the Girdle of Venus are sketchy and broken, the owners can sometimes end up on the wrong side of the law.

SIBLING LINES

There has sometimes been controversy in palmistry where the sibling lines are concerned. Some palmists pay them scant attention, while others will study them in great depth. In Vedic palmistry, the lines are pored over, and they can give current insight as to what is happening to the person's brothers or sisters.

The lines for the siblings are located on the radial side of the hand on the Jupiter Mount edge. If you fold your fingers toward you, you can usually see the lines quite clearly. If the lines are absent, one would assume you would be an only child. Count the number of horizontal lines and it should give an accurate picture of how many siblings there are. Traditional palmists will also refer to the lines to show close relationships, such as half siblings, cousins, and very close friends.

Square on the Sibling Line

The owner's brother or sister might have to go through a difficult period in their lives but will be protected and come out victorious.

Cross

If there is a cross on the sibling line, the person's brother or sister might be hurt in an accident, but if a square surrounds it, then there will be a positive outcome.

Star

The sibling has had a shock.

Grilles

When grilles are present the owner could have a long-running feud with his sibling and they could be estranged. Usually this would be emotional rather than linked to money.

Triangle

This is a good omen as the sibling could come into money and treat his kinfolk to cash to make their lives easier.

Vertical Lines

As a family, there would have been great hardship for all of the siblings, but a close bond would be forged to form a united front.

Purple Dot

This can sometimes mean a sibling is very ill or have a short life span. Another aspect to this formation can be a sibling who might have died at birth or was a late miscarriage.

Extra Lines

If there are extra sibling lines that the subject does not know about on the hand, there might be a secret love child in the background that a parent might not have revealed to the family. A half sibling might have been adopted at birth, or there might have been an affair resulting in a baby that was hushed up. If there is an extra line, this can indicate twins, but one of them may have been lost before, during, or shortly after the birth.

THE QUADRANGLE

(Also called the Angel's Landing Strip)

A Perfect Quadrangle

This should be evenly spaced at each end and at the central point. There should be no marks or blemishes within it other than the passage of the fate line and possibly the Apollo lines; the color should be a medium pink. For true perfection there should be the Mystic Cross standing independently of head and heart line in the center. This represents well-balanced individuals who are stable, loyal, and friendly. Their tolerance levels are high and they will be good listeners with an uncanny knack of judging people correctly.

If the quadrangle is narrow, the person might be intolerant and fond of setting standards for others by being critical and possibly even sarcastic about them. They try to put others right and can be very patronizing and wearing to live with. If the quadrangle is wide, the subject isn't likely to pressurize or criticize others but will leave them to do their own thing. If the head line falls away due to having a deep slope downward, the person might be spiritual, poetic, and rather soft-hearted.

Health

When the quadrangle is wide at each end but narrow in the centre, its owner will have trouble with the lungs, emphysema, and sometimes asthma and chest infections. Heavy smokers can have this configuration and the central quadrangle can be red and inflamed.

If there are many lines, dashes, and crosses in the quadrangle, the subject will be muddled and will have a difficult and problematic life.

Star Burst

If there is a star burst formation in the quadrangle, its owner will have the privilege of seeing something wonderful in their lives. It could be an angel, fairy, spirit, UFO, or other paranormal phenomenon.

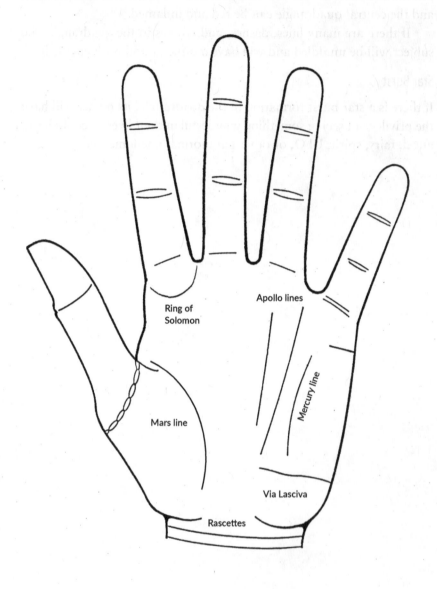

Ring of
Solomon

Apollo lines

Mercury line

Mars line

Via Lasciva

Rascettes

THE MINOR LINES

7

The Minor Lines

There are many minor lines on the hand, and not everyone will have all of them, because each of us is different. The minor lines can be confusing.

TRAVEL LINES

This is an area of palmistry that comes directly from Vedic tradition and it was unknown in the West until about twenty-five years ago. Western palmists have now discovered that it works and have added it to their store of knowledge.

Travel lines appear on the percussion edge of the hand and they show up anywhere from under the Mount of Mercury, just under the heart line, downward (see illustration on page 62). Therefore, they appear on the percussion edge of the Mount of Mars and the Mount of the Moon. Look closely for horizontal lines in this area and carefully add up each line, because each one will represent a journey in the person's life.

The dominant hand holds future information and the nondominant hand usually represents past information for journeys already taken. Some palmists believe if the nondominant hand has many travel lines and the owner hasn't traveled, they will yearn to do so.

Where in the World?

Many years ago, Sasha realized these lines represented important journeys, and she soon found that she could tell which countries her clients had visited in the past or was due to visit in the future.

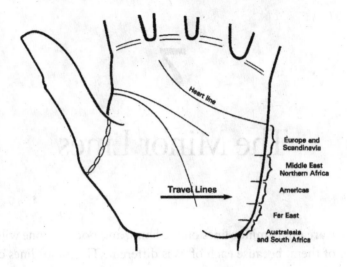

She discussed these findings with an Indian colleague who used the Vedic tradition, and his response amazed her. He rummaged around in his papers and handed her a photocopy of a hand with many fine lines drawn in on the percussion edge, each one marked with the name of a country. The information was much more detailed than the work she had done, but tallied with her own diagnosis.

Cross on a Line

This doesn't bode well, because the person might have a journey that is perilous in some way. If a square is encompassing the cross then the disaster will be averted. Crosses can sometimes represent accidents or broken bones.

One Chain on the Line

An emotional upset that could spoil the journey, so there might be an argument with a traveling companion. My daughter Leanna has this formation and this is how it played out in her life. When she was just seventeen she went on holiday to America with a female friend. When her friend met a would-be lover, she chased after him to a different state, leaving my daughter for over a week, very distressed at being left alone in a strange country.

Loop Chains

Loop chains on a travel line suggest a difficult journey with many obstacles. Suitcases could go missing and accommodation might be disappointing. It can represent one upset after another and the feeling that you need another holiday to recover from the one you have just had! I have this formation on my hand and while in Canada my suitcases were lost for five days. All I had were the clothes on my back and my handbag!

Vertical Lines

Thin red vertical lines on a travel line can represent illness while abroad so the individual can return home with a virus or an upset stomach. If a cross is present on the line, the traveler could spend some time in hospital.

Pentagram

If a pentagram appears on a line of travel, the owner will be really blessed with a stunning holiday or a mind-blowing experience. They may swim with dolphins or perhaps see the aurora borealis, or go trekking in the Amazon Forest.

Three Horizontal Lines

When three lines are linked together, the subject will visit three different locations or perhaps three islands on one visit. This is seen more often due to cruises or coach tours.

A Purple Dot

A purple dot is not a good thing to see on a travel line, as it represents great anxiety or a shock. To be fair, this sign is not often seen on the hand, but, if seen, you can bet your life the person has undergone or will undergo, some terrible ordeal, such as an attack or a robbery or suddenly finding themselves lost and off the beaten track. My nephew has this formation and when he was in Thailand, he was badly bitten by a starving dog. He loves dogs so he was really upset and shocked by the incident for many months.

A Fork

A fork can mean the person will have to make a detour on their journey. I have this mark on my palm, and many years ago the plane I was traveling in had air conditioning problems and we were relocated to another airport until the problem was fixed.

A Half Triangle

When this sign is on a travel line, it is a good omen. Money or riches can be made in a foreign country. If the life line has a fork on it as well, the person might decide to work and live abroad and will enjoy an opulent lifestyle there.

THE VIA LASCIVA

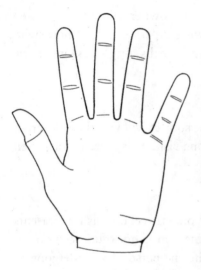

This line used to be called the poison line, or the allergy line. When studied closely, it can give a good diagnosis of the person's health, and it can also be linked to travel. It is not present on everyone's hand.

Broken Via Lasciva

If the Via Lasciva is broken or small and has an island or two present, the owners will struggle with their diet and food intake. They might starve for a week and then binge on all the wrong types of food. Some subjects could have a drinking problem, and this can be seen if the line is red and blotchy.

Long, Clear Via Lasciva

This can represent sensitivity to chemicals and medicines, plus allergies to foods such as peanuts, wheat, etc. I have found that with this type of line, the person is into alternative medicines and systems such as healing, homeopathy, and herbal remedies and will have success in maintaining a healthy lifestyle. The owner may be gifted with healing for others.

THE MARS LINE

The line of Mars lies between the line of life and the thumb and it ends on the Mount of Venus. Push the thumb toward the Jupiter finger and look for a short line on the inside of the life line. Inexperienced palmists can confuse this with another line that is the sister life line or the inner life line, which also sits quite close to the life line, but the line of Mars is a good quarter of an inch away from it. When found, this is classed as very lucky. When seen on both hands this is really special, and if the line is long then the person should have a charmed life.

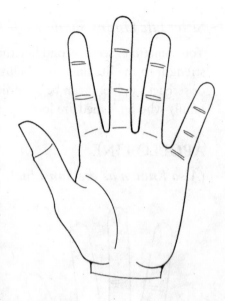

A strong Mars line will represent vitality, strength, and determination. Often this line will be seen in people who are connected to the armed forces and occupations that require bravery such as the fire and rescue services and some types of sport. The owner will be talented in a special way and will often shine in their particular field. In years gone by, this line often showed up on those who were conscripted into the armed services and who thoroughly enjoyed the experience. Now you may find it on the hands of people who enjoyed their time as scouts, guides, and cadets. In short these types enjoy being away from home, being a part of a team, and facing challenges. The owner of a strong Mars line will be blessed with a good constitution and if they do become ill, will get better very quickly.

Fragmented Mars Line

In Vedic palmistry, a broken and fragile line of Mars can denote stomach and digestive disorders. If the line is tasseled or chained then the person could be prone to headaches.

Sister Life Line or Shadow Life Line

You sometimes see a second line that lies close to the life line; this gives strength to the life line, so it helps the individual recover from illness or setbacks in life. It can be an indication that members of the subject's family who have died are looking after them, from the "other side."

APOLLO LINE

(Also Known as the Sun Line)

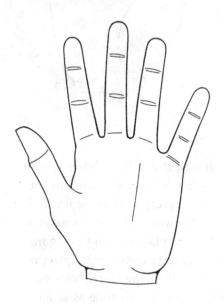

The Apollo line runs up the hand from the wrist end to the finger end, in a similar way to the fate line, but located toward the ulna side of the fate line. It usually commences near the wrist and ascends vertically to the Apollo finger.

This is a brilliant aspect to see as it brings wealth, health, and happiness, and it is said the person should have an idyllic life with many blessings and fame. Needless to say, palmists don't often see a perfect Apollo line. In Vedic palmistry, the owner will have endured many hard past lives, so this time round, they reap the blessings of their past trials and tribulations.

The origins of the Apollo line can vary a great deal and can be confusing, but in time you should get a feel for the procedure. I usually scan the Apollo mount, as there's often something there to help.

Apollo Line Starting Inside the Life Line

This is an unusual formation. It shows the owner will have received lots of help from their family early on, which has helped them succeed in life. The owner will enjoy art and books and will have a keen intellect. This subject can read others in an instant.

Mount of the Moon

When this line ascends from the Moon mount to the Apollo finger, the owner will be gifted in all things pertaining to the arts. This could be writing, acting, dancing, or singing. They will inspire those around them and will have a double dose of charisma and definitely have the X Factor!

Apollo Line on the Plain of Mars

This is easily confused with the fate line and can often be seen running side by side with it. These people will eventually reach their goals, but only with a great deal of personal struggle and determination. They are proud and independent.

Apollo Line Emerging from the Fate Line

Those who have hands that show an Apollo line connecting half way up the hand will succeed in the arts. These subjects will have strokes of good luck that help them on their journey. If they change tack and go after a completely different type of career later in life, that will also be successful.

Apollo Line Ending on the Heart Line

Although the owner will be driven to succeed, their emotional immaturity will hold them back. There will be wasted talent and lost opportunities, and this type will often have excuses for their lack of success and will constantly blame others.

Apollo Line Ending on the Head Line

This is not a wonderful placement, because the owner will have real struggles in life through their lack of judgment. They find it hard to change their opinions and listen to reason. As far as finances are concerned, it could be bad news, with bankruptcy on the agenda.

Apollo Line on the Apollo Mount

Even if this is the only part of the Apollo Line in evidence, the news is good, as it points to happiness in later life and an enjoyable old age.

THE MERCURY LINE

(Also Known as the Hepatic Line)

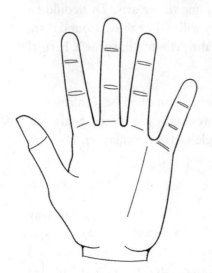

We look at this line to give an indication of the person's health and stamina because the stronger the line, the stronger the person is. A thin broken Mercury line signifies a weak constitution. If you want to know if your client is stressed, a broken small line is a good indicator that they are under pressure and need to chill out.

The Medical Striata

The Medical Striata is the name of a small group of lines located on the Mercury Mount just above the heart line. There are often three little lines that rise up in a slightly diagonal direction, often with another line crossing them in a slanting direction. However there can be as many as seven vertical lines. These marks show a very special gift and can be seen in the palms of spiritual healers, homeopaths, and those practicing complementary medicines. They are also present on the hands of nurses, midwives, vets, doctors, and dentists. I have a friend who is a psychologist, and she has these marks very clearly on her hand.

When looking at younger people's hands, the Striata can indicate that they will go into a life of medical service, and Vedic palmistry suggests that the child is gifted, with many blessings. It can also represent a wiser soul reincarnating to ease the burdens of others.

As the left hand is what destiny gives you and the right hand what you do with it, both hands must be looked at closely. If the medical striata are in the left hand but not the right, the person has blocked the gift in some way, and it can be a palmist's duty to remind them of their gift.

Moles, Warts, and Blemishes

When looking at palms, you will sometimes see warts and skin eruptions, and these can give away mysterious secrets.

Warts are classed as a blockage, and the owner will have to work through the things in the area of that block. For example, if there is a large mole on the Mount of Venus, the person will be prone to making huge mistakes in love.

Temporary red patches show a shock, an illness, a worry, or some other problem that has arisen around the time of the reading. The redness will go once the problem passes.

part four

THE
FINGERS

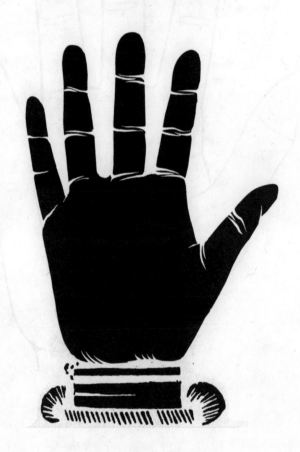

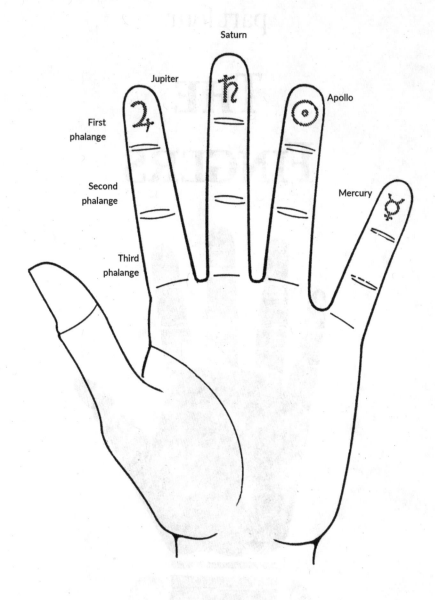

THE MAP OF THE FINGERS

8

The Phalanges

Fingers are comprised of phalanges—when you bend your fingers you will notice three distinct segments. Every one of us has phalanges on our fingers. All are unique, and they can give us a great deal of insight into a person's character. The bottom phalange is nearest to the palm and then comes the middle one, with the top one being the phalange that bears the fingertips.

- The Top Phalange relates to mental abilities and the way we think about our lives.

- The Middle Phalange relates to practicality and the way we apply ourselves.

- The Bottom Phalange relates to basic needs, comfort, and materialism.

Perfect Phalanges

These will be equal in length with no grilles, crosses, or blemishes. The owners will be well balanced and successful in most walks of life. They will be hard working, kind, and spiritual.

Thumb Phalanges

There are usually only two phalanges for the thumb. Sometimes there can be a third but this is not often seen. The top phalange of the thumb represents willpower, the second phalange concerns logic. A third phalange would indicate an unusual type of person.

Long Top Phalanges

Long top phalanges usually belong to the spiritual type of person, so philosophy, religion, and metaphysical interests will be high on their agenda. They will be good at psychoanalyzing others, often scanning them with accuracy. On the down side, these people have to be careful not to become isolated or to withdraw into their own worlds, because the gifts they have been given must be shared with others to help them to understand themselves more fully. They make excellent psychiatrists, clairvoyants, or reformers of society, so they can have a profound impact on those who come into their circle. Health wise, their nerves can sometime be a problem, and they must remember to eat properly!

Long Middle Phalanges

The owners of this type of phalange will be intellectual, witty, and positive. They will often go into higher education as they get older, maybe taking a degree or going into teaching. The world is their oyster, as their heads rule their hearts. They are law abiding and responsible and often take their attitude of responsibility into their place of work. The best professions for them could be medicine, science, business, and law.

Long Bottom Phalanges

If all the bottom phalanges are longer than the other two, the owner's characteristics will be down to earth, and he will deal with practical aspects of life very well, perhaps coming into the spiritual areas when he is older. His physical abilities will be strong, and hard work won't frighten him, as he will have plenty of energy for building, farming, gardening, and manual tasks. He prefers to follow rather than to lead and won't really enjoy being self-employed. If the palm is a fire palm, then self-employment is more likely. This person likes to be comfortable, both in the financial sense and in the sense of having a comfortable sofa and bed to relax into.

Short Top Phalanges

These people need to push themselves to study because learning and knowledge doesn't come easily to them. Even when reading a book, they will skim the pages or look into the back of the book for the ending. When doing a reading for this type, it is best to encourage them to take their time and be patient and then the small tasks will eventually become easier for them.

Short Middle Phalanges

When the middle phalanges are short there will be a need to stretch the mind to improve on practical skills. Often this type will go on to be quite creative, but will need to develop patience and perseverance. They will want things done quickly, and they are inclined to be slapdash and untidy.

Short Bottom Phalanges

This type is inclined to be very materialistic, and they can make money their god. If they are not wealthy, they must take care not to get into debt. They will love the latest fashion accessories and gadgets and will like to keep up with the Joneses. The owners will need to bring action into their careers, as they can get stuck in a rut, staying in the same job for years.

Four Phalanges

This is an unusual thing to see, but when it does appear, it's most likely to be on the Mercury finger where it means that the person is good with figures, statistics, and accountancy. This person could make a career in banking, or he may spend his working life dealing with contracts, legacies, and mortgages. He could even spend some part of his life as an editor, designer, typesetter, or formatter for publishing businesses. All this is really due to an aptitude for details and for reading meaning into statistics. He would make a good staff officer in the army where an understanding of logistics is the key to success. This person could become wealthy and then spend time or money helping charities. He is kind, courteous, and fun loving.

Two Phalanges

Again this is a rare thing to see on anything other than the thumb. When it does appear, it's usually on the Mercury finger, but it could turn up on any finger. This subject has a good grasp of science, especially if the top phalange is the longer, and he may become quite famous whereby his pioneering skills could be a great help to science or medicine. If the lower phalange is the longer, the owner will have good commercial acumen. However, he will be very artistic and creative, and he should be encouraged to use this more.

Fat or Thin Phalanges

Pleasantly plump top phalanges refer to a person who needs financial security and who likes to save money for a rainy day. He also craves secure relationships and will put a great deal of effort into marriage and family life. If all of the phalanges are plump, and especially if the fat is hard-packed, the individual may be fond of food and drink, and he could have a lazy disposition.

Slim Phalanges

Slim phalanges belong on an active person who won't be easy going, as he has a nervous and restless disposition. Slim phalanges on the thumb represent a gentle soul who wants others to like him. He doesn't have much energy and he prefers not to do too much hard work.

The Jupiter Finger

This is probably the most important finger, as it relates to the person's ego, will, and desire for success, along with leadership qualities and business or teaching ability. It has extremely strong connections to spirituality, and that is especially the case for the top (fingertip) phalange. I have gone into this finger in more detail than the others.

9

Reading the Fingers

Fingers that are quite long in proportion to the palm denote intellectual ability and mental power. When short and stubby looking, the subject is inclined to hold back, and may take longer to absorb and learn things; having said that, there are plenty of classical and modern musicians, composers, and writers who have fingers shorter than their palms. They have fire hands, and as such are creative individuals.

Bear in mind that the way the fingers are set on the hand can make them appear short, so use a ruler when comparing one finger with another.

- The index finger is called the finger of Jupiter.

- The middle finger is called the finger of Saturn.

- The ring finger is called the finger of the Sun or Apollo

- The little finger is called the finger of Mercury.

JUPITER FINGER

The Jupiter finger represents the person themself, the ego, and the things they believe in, along with such things as leadership qualities and strength of character. The finger of Jupiter represents social consciousness, idealism, and careers. When long, it means the owner could be in business for themselves and in charge of their own company or even a chain of companies. If short, it denotes a lack of confidence, a dislike of responsibility and no ambition. The person will prefer to melt into the background. When the finger is medium in length, then we will see a balanced individual.

Jupiter Finger—Top Phalange

A vertical line

A vertical line here represents upstanding individuals who will always keep their word. If something needs doing, they will set about the task and achieve completion. They are always aware of their spiritual and psychic nature and try to live an honest life. As they are in the later stages of reincarnation, they influence and touch the hearts of those they meet.

A cross

In Vedic palmistry, there is a lot of superstition concerning a cross on the top phalange of Jupiter. Some say it is the mark of the devil, while others will say the owners will never achieve anything good in their lives and will subsequently ruin the lives of those around them. These individuals can lack vision and be young souls.

A star

A star with five points is a very good mark. It indicates the owners have a real mission in life and will help to improve the lives of others. These people become important and gain many spiritual rewards during their lifetimes. They have great wisdom and empathy with people, and a real understanding of the animal kingdom.

Two stars

One star is an uncommon formation but two stars are exceedingly rare. This mark belongs on the hands of those who are really old souls, who have great God-given wisdom. They can often be holy men, gurus, and Mother Theresa types who will make a difference all over the world with their insight and knowledge.

A triangle

A triangle is an unusual mark and it should be perfectly formed so there is no mistake. This can be the sign of those who have been gifted with magic. High priestesses, mediums, or theosophists might have this mark as they are interested in all things pertaining to the spiritual or occult. They will live a good life and will certainly enlighten and inspire those they meet.

A square

The square represents protection from danger.

A circle

A circle is an uncommon mark that is a very good formation to have here. These folk will achieve tremendous things in their lives, and even when there is great struggle, they will succeed because they have a deep belief in life and a strong faith in spiritual or religious matters.

An island

An island that is shaped like a crumpled leaf is not always a good sign. These individuals can get sidetracked in life. They won't think much about their spirituality and rarely achieve anything significant. Often they will take the easy path and hate to strive hard.

Dashes

Dashes on any of the top phalanges can represent fatigue for the individual. This is also a sign of stress at work or personal life. If the lines are red, we can assume their problems are recent. If the lines are faded, the events might have just passed.

A grille

A grille looks a little like a bit of woven cloth and is not a positive sign. The person may not have any faith or religion, and may lean too much on others.

Wavy lines

Wavy lines denote ambition. These people appear pleasant and they have many friends, but they may have a ruthless streak.

Dots

Dots or pitting on the tips of the fingers can indicate an underlying health problem, especially if there are dashes as well. The person's nerves could be bad and he could be suffering from acute fatigue. Sometimes you might advise the person to rest or have a good holiday to balance things out.

Jupiter Finger—Middle Phalange

A vertical line

This person will achieve much in life and will be well liked and respected. He has the interests of others at heart and he will make a good parent, partner, or boss.

A horizontal line

This subject can change his mind at the drop of a hat.

A wavy line

A wavy line here represents ambition and a desire for recognition, along with a tendency to get others to do the work for the subject. He may have too many irons in the fire.

A cross

A cross can indicate potential success with writing or anything creative.

A star

A star is the mark of a saint or holy person who has wisdom and clarity of vision. Others seek him out to gain insight, even though the subject won't necessarily want to be in the public eye.

A square

A square foretells determination, strength, and a driven nature. These types succeed in all they put their minds to. They make enemies, but as this is a sign of protection, they will be saved from any real danger or from the envy of others.

A circle

A circle is the mark of success and a good and happy life. If these people are interested in art, their work could become well known.

A grille

These folk may have difficulty in keeping friends or relationships, and they may need help in becoming good parents.

Jupiter Finger—Bottom Phalange

A vertical Line

A vertical line here belongs on those who try hard to improve their personalities, and they don't allow their physical and worldly needs to control them. If there are multiple lines, they will make real headway and get to the top.

Wavy lines

This person tries hard to improve a difficult nature, but he never forgets a hurt.

Slanting lines

Slanting lines can indicate an inheritance and a wealthy lifestyle for the owner. This lucky person gets to enjoy the finest things and he may buy a holiday home abroad. He needs to watch his weight and his food intake as he can overdo things and damage his health.

A cross

A cross belongs on the hands of those who lack savoir-faire and who can upset others by their lack of finesse.

A star

A star here is a sign of someone who may not always keep promises.

A square

I have seen this on younger folk who have had bad parents and no real guidance. They often have to bring themselves up or set their own standards.

A circle

A circle is one of the better marks to have on the bottom phalange and it denotes success.

A grille

A grille can show a fondness for drugs or drink.

SATURN FINGER

The finger of Saturn represents trends, psychology, and is sometimes called the finger of destiny. When long, it can mean prudence, a love of solitude, and reserve. These people need peace and quiet and will love to study. When the Saturn finger is short, it denotes careless frivolity and a lack of seriousness in the person's life. Subjects with medium length Saturn fingers are balanced in all things.

This finger relates to commonsense, ambition, achievement, scientific ability, mathematical ability, and success after a period of hard work. It seems to refer to putting down strong foundations in order to build something that will last. Thus, marks here can denote struggles and hardship but also achievement as a result of keeping going.

Saturn Finger—Top Phalange

A vertical line

Sadness and melancholy, also possible self-absorption.

A cross

A lack of spirituality.

Wavy lines

Wavy lines indicate a lack of discipline and foresight.

A triangle

A triangle here brings success in love and career matters.

A star

Although these people may be in danger at times, they are protected, especially if there is a square around the star.

A circle

A circle is the best sign to have and represents a spiritual and mystical individual who will have great knowledge of things unseen. This is a very rare mark.

A square

A square is a sign of protection, so the individual usually lands on his feet.

A grille

A grille can mean disloyalty or a period of unhappiness.

Saturn Finger—Middle Phalange

A vertical line

A strong clear vertical line is a good omen, representing great wisdom. This is a rare mark and I haven't come across it in my career.

A horizontal line

Horizontal lines denote laziness or temporary obstructions by others.

A cross

These are daring types who love to travel. Check the travel lines on the percussion side of the hand to see if there are any indications of troublesome journeys.

A star

In Vedic palmistry, a star is an unfortunate and rare mark, which can denote a serious accident, but it may be better not to tell the client this.

A square

A square on the middle phalange can be a warning to its owner to be careful and not take any chances, but while these folk are protected, it would be better for them not to tempt fate.

A circle

A circle is the sign of the psychic who could gain huge success and fame. In Vedic palmistry, this will be an old soul who has reincarnated to help others.

A triangle

A triangle is a rare mark and belongs on the hands of those who have a talent for psychic and magical matters. They love to study all things esoteric and will search deeply for the meanings of life, becoming visionaries and healers.

A grille

A grille indicates anxiety, so this person would benefit from meditation, hypnotherapy, and counseling.

Saturn Finger—Bottom Phalange

A vertical line

A vertical line denotes courage and success in the law or the armed forces. A mass of vertical lines suggests careers that put the person in contact with the earth, such as horticulture, farming, or mining. They are hard workers so they earn good money, but they may be loners.

A slanting fork

Slanting forks depict characters that are hard to please, critical, and fault finding. They can be lonely in old age.

A cross

On a woman's hand, a cross represents fertility problems, so you must also check the first Rascette of Venus to see if that is arched, because she might need fertility treatment.

Horizontal lines

Horizontal lines show those who are solitary and shy.

A grille

Grilles here belong on the hands of those with oodles of cash but they aren't generous with it.

A star

A star denotes a practical problem that is probably temporary.

A triangle

This denotes a love of learning and an aptitude for science.

A square

A square is a wonderful sign of protection against poverty.

A circle

A circle shows an ability to shine in the fields of research, science, and philosophy. These special people are leading lights and will help to pioneer new things.

SUN FINGER OR APOLLO FINGER

When long, it gives the owner a love of beauty and the desire for celebrity, status, and fame. The owner will like the arts, music, antiques, museums, and ancient castles. They also love children and delight in helping them to grow through teaching. When excessively long, the ego will be large and the owner will like notoriety and will take risks when speculating. They will love money and perhaps gambling. Recent medical research shows a long Apollo finger owner will have a talent for engineering, technical drawing, and computer software design. These folk can also be extremely clever with dress design and manufacture.

Apollo Finger—Top Phalange

A vertical line

Sadness.

Wavy lines

A lack of self-discipline and a disinclination to listen to others.

A cross

Luck with windfalls and inheritances.

A star

These folk learn the meaning of destiny and they have a cathartic impact upon others.

A triangle

These natives can charm the birds out of the trees.

A square

This person doesn't display good judgment when choosing his friends.

A circle

These people strive hard to improve themselves and want to gather as much information as possible on subjects such as healing, clairvoyance, and spiritual work. This is a sign of success and spiritual advancement.

A grille

The grille shows poor judgment.

Apollo Finger—Middle Phalange

A vertical line

A vertical line here is always nice to see, as the person will have a good heart and will be extremely kind.

Horizontal lines

A restless and rather shallow nature, they can't sit still or think deeply.

A thick slanting line

This can be an indicator of bad health to come. Check out other areas of the hand to confirm this. In ancient Vedic palmistry, this was considered to be a line of poison and treachery!

A cross

A cross here shows a daredevil nature and a fondness for challenging sports. They mix with like-minded friends and rarely settle for more serious pursuits.

A star

A temporary problem.

A square

These people shouldn't take chances.

A triangle

A triangle is a good sign, as these subjects are conscientious.

A circle

These individuals have a feel for future world events and they will be ahead of their time. Their predictions often come true.

A grille

A grille here can indicate ill luck, trials, and tribulations. I often feel that these people are using their current incarnation to learn the lessons of three lives simultaneously.

Apollo Finger—Bottom Phalange

A vertical line

This denotes courage.

A slanting line

A slanting line is rare and can be seen on a military person's hand.

Multiple vertical lines

This person is tired or downhearted, but the situation is temporary.

Horizontal lines

These natives don't have a strong grip on reality.

A cross

A cross can signify a fertility problem. If on a man's hand, a low sperm count can be a possibility, or in modern-day palmistry, he might have undergone a vasectomy.

A star

A star doesn't augur well, and it can relate to violence in the home.

A triangle

A triangle represents clever types who have scientific brains but their friends can let them down.

A square

This person may feel that he is lacking something in his life at the time of the reading.

A circle

A circle suggests individuals who are working in research and scientific study. They have an air of authority and will gain great respect from others through their career.

A grille

These folk love money—maybe a little too much.

THE MERCURY FINGER

If long, it represents mental power, eloquence, and a grasp of languages and a fondness for scientific studies. The subject will be a great communicator and lecturer. When short, it denotes a difficulty in the spoken word and in the expression of thoughts. When crooked or turned in, secrecy will be present in their nature. A pointed Mercury finger can denote a psychic ability, especially if the other fingers are not pointed.

Mercury Finger—Top Phalange

A vertical line

These owners will do well in most things in life; they have inventive minds, and are they are often ahead of the game. These folk gain recognition and fame, and they may use their psychic abilities to enhance their lives.

Horizontal lines

Horizontal lines suggest the individual could be prone to jealousy or he may think a lot of himself.

A cross

A cross gives these types the gift of eloquence, and they can captivate an audience. They will be highly intuitive and able to see into the future.

A star

A star is a good sign, as the owners will have the gift for oration, teaching, and lecturing.

A triangle

A triangle is a very special mark that indicates real psychic ability.

A square

This person will go into the deeper aspects of psychic work and could become a medium or astrologer.

A circle

A circle is a positive sign for eloquence, popularity, and success in media work.

A grille

This shows a deceptive nature and someone who may not keep promises.

Mercury Finger—Middle phalange

A vertical line

A vertical line reveals a talent for science, technology, and research.

Horizontal lines

Horizontal lines denote a series of blockages. These folk have sharp minds and a talent for science, but they may face delays in their careers or lives.

A cross

A cross on a bent in Mercury finger can show criminal tendencies.

A star

A star belongs to a sharp operator.

A triangle

A triangle is a very special mark, and the owners, after scientific work and exploration, will turn to the psychic and esoteric sciences later on in life and become quite psychic.

A square

A square warns of dishonesty, but the person can straighten himself out in time.

A circle

A circle denotes honor for unusual and outstanding scientific work.

A grille

This person can blunder from one mistake to another.

A mass of vertical lines

A mass of vertical lines indicates hard work and overcoming difficulties in life. This also represents wisdom that comes with spiritual enlightenment.

Mercury Finger—Bottom Phalange

Vertical lines

This shows a struggle in life that may be a result of karma, but later life is better.

A mass of vertical lines

This person is temporarily short of money.

Horizontal lines

Horizontal lines represent temptations.

A cross

A cross shows the need for a good father figure or counselor.

A star

A star is rare for the bottom phalanges of Mercury, and I have only seen it once or twice in my career. The owners have the gift of eloquence and will captivate their audiences. They can be wonderful speakers and have creative natures, which will bring them blessings of success.

A triangle

A triangle is a good omen and the owners will have a lot of influence on others. They may become judges, barristers, or diplomats, because their negotiating abilities are exceptional.

A grille

Grilles suggest that the subject can be shady. He is a young soul.

A square

Secrecy.

A circle

An enterprising nature and a desire to help others.

10

Inclination

The way the fingers lean is interesting, and this is something you can even spot at a distance without the person being aware of your interest.

Restricted—No Gaps between Fingers

People who have this kind of hand often appear very outgoing, but this

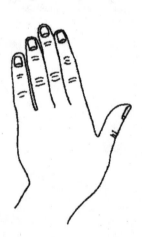

is in contrast to their true nature. Indeed some are wonderful sales people and others are politicians or very public figures, but they are not what they seem. These subjects are extremely private and introverted. They may have lacked attention in their childhood, which has left them feeling insecure. They need to feel completely in control of their lives. Their love relationships can be strained because they are possessive, due to their fear that their partner might stray. Politicians with hands that don't allow any light to shine through the fingers won't want to listen to the opinions of others.

Cash wise, these folk can be tight fisted. They will make sure they have everything they want, but will deny others any luxuries.

Inwardly Inclining Fingers

This is an unusual formation, and one that will not often be seen. There are two possibilities here: the first is that these people are very interesting, but hard to read for, because they are secretive and on their guard.

These individuals trust no one and prefer others to fight their battles for them. Often they will feel the grass is greener on the other side of the hill. They need to get pleasure from making money from their crafts or hobbies.

The second possibility is their having some kind of mental handicap, perhaps including Down syndrome.

Space between Jupiter and Saturn

These people will always follow the dictates of their hearts. They will be good workers and often have their own business in which they succeed, but they are not clever when it comes to personal relationships. This may be due to a selfish streak. Success is more important than love.

Saturn and Apollo Leaning
Toward Each Other

This is quite a common arrangement. These subjects will need a lot of understanding and security because they have fragile egos. They must also have job satisfaction, which they will prefer to lots of money.

Saturn and Apollo Leaning
Away From Each Other

These people are rather lonely and they daydream about the past. When they are down, they can be rebellious and difficult at home or work. They find it hard to face the future or plan ahead and hate being the center of attention, because of their shyness. Once they are settled and happy, with family and good friendships, their natural sense of humor and goodwill shines through.

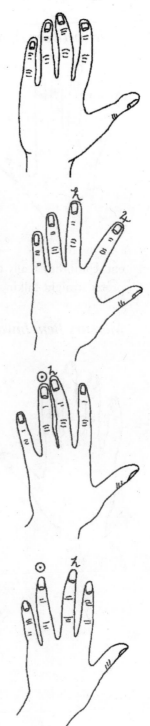

Space between Apollo and Mercury

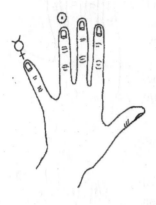

This is a common sight, although the spacing can vary from a small gap to a very large one.

These people are very intuitive and can sometimes read the minds of others. Inwardly, they are quite lonely and like their own space. If they don't have space, they could feel suffocated and nervous. In relationships, their partner must understand their need for independence and freedom. They won't rush into new relationships, as they are cautious about love. This hand type makes an excellent parent. Until they really trust someone, they are not easily influenced. They prefer straight-talking people.

Mercury Bent Inward

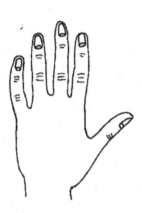

Traditional palmists considered this a negative sign, with the owner being judged as manipulative, dishonest, and secretive, especially where money matters are concerned. Some modern palmists look on this in a very different way, seeing the owner as the soul of discretion who will never divulge the secrets of others. This being the case, they can make excellent counselors. As there is controversy about this formation, it is up to the individual palmist to decide, depending on the severity of the incline.

11

Fingertips

In your reading, pay attention to the fingertips, as the shape has much to add to your overall reading of the hands.

Spatulate Fingertips

Spatulate or splayed fingertips have an alien look about them and represent an active type of person who loves to be in the thick of things. In spite of this, these people crave open spaces. They are restless souls who are easily bored. Their minds are scientific and energetic. Often these people are inventive and ahead of their time, especially if they have the astrological sign of Aquarius.

Careers

These types would be happy as explorers, inventors, scientists, architects, barristers, industrial engineers, or members the armed forces and emergency services. They like electronics.

In Love

To be totally happy in a relationship, these individuals must be allowed freedom. Partners must understand their wish to travel and explore. Their inventive minds are always seeking new thrills. They don't like to stay at home to raise a family, and will hate to be trapped in a mundane job. For the marriage to survive with this type, it would be best to have exactly the same interests.

Health

These individuals suffer from nervous tension and muscle strain.

Rounded Fingertips

These people will put up with things for a long time, because they don't like to say no. Their souls are pure and hate to see ugliness or discord. In the home, they will be fussy about their decor and color schemes. They have such a sweet disposition that they can be inclined to believe everything they hear, and they are far too trusting. Once they have been let down, they are cautious and find it hard to forgive.

Careers

Careers might include artists, interior designers, teachers, writers, and dress designers. They are very good at accounting and bookkeeping.

In Love

These individuals are madly romantic and won't want to be alone. They like quiet evenings in with a good bottle of wine and a DVD. They remain faithful in love and are excellent parents.

Health

As this type hates any sort of confrontation, they will often suffer with their nerves and have to take care with insomnia.

Square Fingertips

These no-nonsense types get straight to the point, so you will always know where you stand. They like routine, have their feet firmly planted on the ground, and will put in a good day's work for a good day's pay. They don't mind long hours, will be punctual and conscientious, and make fair-minded bosses. One thing is for sure, we need this type, as they make the wheels go around and see things get done properly.

Careers

They can make good bankers, accountants, lawyers, business people, teachers, cooks, and teachers.

Male in Love

This man is very fair and will respond to a clean house, meals that are produced on time, and fresh laundry in the drawer. For this, he will work hard and provide for his family. He may be a little Victorian in his outlook, but his love is long-lasting and he will have old-fashioned manners. He won't forget birthdays and anniversaries, and he will be generous and tender, especially if he has an earth sign such as Taurus, Capricorn, or Virgo.

Female in Love

She will be a homemaker and adore children, especially as she has endless patience. The home will be spotless and run like clockwork, with home-cooked food on the table. She will have a strong traditional streak where her family will take precedence.

Health

Usually this type has a robust constitution and will enjoy a long and healthy life. However, poring over documents and spending long hours in front of the computer might result in eye problems.

Conic Fingertips

This is a blend of rounded and pointed fingers. The owners will be quick minded and alert, literally missing nothing, and with their shrewd nature, will be able to see through others in a nanosecond. Their sensitivity is second to none and they will often be psychic, especially if they have Scorpio strongly emphasized in their charts. Their temperamental nature can be off-putting, as they change from day to day. Sometimes they lack stamina and will really love their creature comforts, especially if the base pads are plump. The conic type will be very kind to animals.

Career

These types could be musicians, yoga teachers, clairvoyants, and veterinary workers.

In Love

Conic types are a little lazy in love, but never boring. Their partners won't know with whom they are going to wake up each morning, because of their multifaceted personalities. What was said yesterday won't mean a thing today, so life will be a merry-go-round. If their partner should stray, then you will see the sparks fly, as these subjects have mercurial tempers and a quick, spiteful tongue. On the positive side, they are great fun and often laugh their partners into bed. Sometimes they will love animals more than people.

Health

Conic owners can be prone to nervousness and digestive disorders. If the Jupiter phalanges are plump, over indulgence can be a problem.

Pointed Fingertips

These people are often glamorous and artistic, with a flair for fashion. You can find them rummaging around in charity shops and trunk sales looking for something different, and they love a bargain! I have often found with this type that they are inclined to be self possessed and critical of others. They will tell you what needs doing, but will they actually get off their backsides and do it themselves? If crossed, they never forget or forgive.

Career

These people can be fund-raisers, fashion sales people, hairdressers, and beauticians.

In Love

These types are dreamers. To them, the chase is usually better than the real thing. They enjoy being wined and dined, but once the passion has worn off, they look around for another romantic challenge. They need a strong partner who will take a no-nonsense approach with them. As parents, they will inspire their young and lavish time on them.

Health

These individuals lack stamina and get tired quickly, so they should take power naps to restore their energy.

Mixed Fingertips

People with mixed fingertips can have more than one career in their lifetime. They may have worked for years in the building trade and end up being a vet or a lay preacher. These types will never be boring, as they will have a go at anything, and their hobbies will be just as diverse. They will enjoy sports, painting, singing, and so on.

Careers

Anything!

In Love

These people are flirtatious, as they love variety. They are good in bed and will experiment with enthusiasm. I find with this type that they never stay in one marriage, because they can be easily tempted. As parents, they will be good fun and will involve the children in all sorts of hobbies.

Health

These types are usually robust and their minds stay forever young.

Droplet Fingertips

This formation isn't often seen on a person's hand. The pads of the fingers are slightly bulbous and fleshy. It's best to slightly curl the fingers and raise the hand to eye level to see the effect to its best effect.

The person who has this type of fingertip will be very shrewd and will strive for perfection. Anything out of place will annoy these folks. They are artistic and extremely psychic. They are acutely aware of energetic atmospheres and will be difficult to fool. Some might say they have a cynical nature, but my belief is they can see ahead and strip away any preconceived ideas that others might have.

Careers

These individuals might take up tarot, mediumship, or counseling. Their love of art and creativity means they might pursue a career in fashion. They can make good beauticians, hair stylists, interior designers, and massage therapists. They are often excellent dressmakers, knitters, or craft workers, with a wonderful sense of touch. As their touch is so sensitive, they might be drawn to things as diverse as fine carpentry, decorative cake-craft, or dress design.

In Love

These people are hard to please, since they can more or less read their partner's mind. They have very high standards, so they won't waste time on endless affairs, but would prefer to wait for a soulmate to come along.

12

Fingerprints

Every person has a unique set of fingerprints, and fingerprints have a long history of being used as a form of identification. The ancient Babylonians often used fingerprints on clay tablets as a signature for their business transactions, and the ancient Chinese used thumbprints on clay seals. The human fingerprint is fully formed inside the womb at around sixteen weeks, and it's composed of between fifty and a hundred lines.

The use of fingerprinting by the police as a way of identifying criminals started in 1903 in the USA, and since then the method has been used all over the world.

The study of skin-ridge patterns, or fingerprints, is called dermatoglyphics. This word is derived from *derma*, meaning skin, and *glyph*, meaning carving or design. There are five different types of fingerprint: whorls, arches, tented arches, loops, and peacock's eye.

Fingerprint Patterns

Whorls—Fire Element

WHORL ON JUPITER

These people will be artistic and independent and strive to run their own businesses. They are very shrewd and nothing gets past them. As youngsters, they lack the carefree attitudes of their peer group, because they can see through situations and are wise beyond their years. They often put their own parents under the microscope.

WHORL ON SATURN

If they respect someone, these folk will listen to and even motivate them into trying new things. They are nosy and love to get to the bottom of secrets and subterfuge. They have brilliant organizational skills and do everything to perfection.

WHORL ON APOLLO

These folk have moods that can swing from high to low within a few hours and they can be irritated if things are not just so. They hate untidiness and ugliness of any kind, and if they are partnered with a lazy mate, the marriage will seldom work.

WHORL ON MERCURY

Often people with this fingerprint will be quiet, retiring, and self conscious, and will need motivating, but once they get started on their given subject, they can rattle on for hours. They have an eagle eye, and will soon spot if something isn't right. Where spiritual faith is concerned, they will look into a variety of beliefs.

WHORL ON VENUS (THE THUMB)

Stomach or digestive disorders can be a problem for this type. They will have strong leadership gifts and love to be in charge. Usually they will make a good job of things because of their wonderful organizational skills. As a parent, they need to be less authoritarian and more easy-going.

Arches—Earth element

These are down-to-earth types who are the salt of the earth, very trustworthy and have good common sense. They will not believe anything unless they actually have proof. If the arches are on all fingers, this might indicate chromosomal abnormalities. On the negative side, they tend to have low self-esteem.

ARCH ON JUPITER

This type of fingerprint on Jupiter will bring frustration, and the owner will be inclined to bottle things up. They also suffer with self-esteem issues. They save their money and will make sure there is a good investment plan for their future.

ARCH ON SATURN

The owner of this fingerprint will want to study, pass exams, and gain knowledge. They are traditionalists, so they value older friends and take time to accept new ideas. They try to manipulate others.

ARCH ON APOLLO

These types keep their feelings hidden, maintaining the British "stiff upper lip." They hate others to be over emotional and will often push things from their past into the deepest recesses of their mind.

ARCH ON MERCURY

They enjoy tradition; they will not seek to change or rethink their own ideas, and so they become behind the times.

ARCH ON VENUS—THE THUMB

The owner will be practical and honest; what you see is what you get. This person will definitely have a domineering streak. They are passionate, but they can be blind to the faults of those whom they love.

Tented Arches—Air element

This is a formation with an upright central core. It is usually found on the Jupiter finger. People with this fingerprint can be highly-strung and sensitive and will strive to seek the truth in all matters. They usually have a hyperactive and fiery nature. It is rare to see the formation on all fingers, but if so, the person will love music and artistic projects.

Loops—Water element

 This is the most common variety of fingerprint. Loop formations can come in from either side of the finger, although those that come from the thumb or radial side of the finger are less common than the ulna loops. Radial loops mainly appear on the Jupiter finger, but they can turn up on other fingers. Subjects with radial loops have stronger personalities than those with ulna loops. When on Jupiter, they have leadership qualities, will be bossy, and will want their own way. Ulna loop people are flexible, sociable, and reasonable.

The owner of any loop print has many irons in the fire. Their gift is to be unique, and they will often have ideas that are ahead of their time. They prefer to let others lead. If the loops are present on all fingers, then the individual will be very well balanced.

LOOP ON JUPITER

These people have good potential to be self-employed and successful in their chosen career.

LOOP ON SATURN

This type is usually inventive with a strong creative streak. They can make something out of nothing, and, because of their unique approach, they will always be ahead of the game.

LOOP ON APOLLO

This subject will be hard to understand and will spend much time on self analysis. Unless this person has lived through a certain problem, he will not be able to empathize with the emotions of others. The old expression comes to mind that you cannot teach what you haven't learned.

LOOP ON MERCURY

This is a rare formation, and the person that has it will have radical views on religion and all things spiritual. Their concepts are modern and visionary and they seem to be able instinctively to know the truth. If you believe in reincarnation, this person would be classed as an old soul.

• •
LOOP ON VENUS

This type is usually more submissive than analytical or creative, and will usually work for someone else rather than running their own business.

Double Loop

This person can see both sides of the story and can be a good mediator. They contemplate long and hard before making a decision. This print is usually found on the Jupiter finger or the thumb (Venus). The person is practical and into the material world, and can be a little inflexible.

When the double loop is small and tight, the person will be intuitive, but the intuition will confuse them, as they try to use logic instead of their gut feeling.

Peacock's Eye

This is a rare fingerprint. Its owner will be a perfectionist with an excellent eye for detail. In Vedic palmistry, this was also known as a sign of a magic person or a visionary. If it appears on the Apollo finger, the owner will be gifted in the arts and if on the Saturn finger, the person will be creative in things like carpentry, metalwork, engineering, or sculpture. A Peacock's Eye on the mercury finger signifies an excellent writer or teacher.

13

Fingernails

Fingernails are made of a protein called keratin. If the nail is damaged or torn off completely, it will take between six and eight months to grow back. Hippocrates remarked that the nail reflects the condition of the body. We can find out a great deal about a person's character from the nail shape. The first things a good palmist will want to study are the fingernails, because there is a wealth of information displayed on them, especially concerning health. The texture, color, and shape of the nail must be taken into careful consideration.

Hard or Soft Nails

Nails tend to harden with age, and as many older people have discovered, toenails can become very difficult to cut in later life. However, those with hard nails are usually careful with money. They may or may not earn good money, but they tend not to overspend.

Soft nails can denote poor health, but also a self-indulgent nature, or just that the individual is in a phase of overspending. If your nails are normally all right but suddenly start flaking or becoming soft, examine your health and your bank balance!

Nail Shapes

The nail generally has a variation of one of five shapes: broad, oval, short, square, and narrow. Healthy nails will be a pale pink color with a decent moon at the bed of the nail and a slight bloom or sheen on them.

Broad, Square Nails

People with broad, square nails have stamina and drive and will enjoy good health. Their faults are stubbornness and a need to be in charge. These folk have boundless energy and optimism and usually succeed in all they do. They tend to not sit still, and their restless nature can sometimes be annoying to gentler souls.

They are prone to small and silly accidents. They might also suffer with tension to the shoulders and neck.

Narrow Nails

The owners of these nails have little stamina and a nervous temperament. Their spirit will lack courage, and they could be apprehensive about even the smallest problems. One of their main faults is that they don't finish what they have started. They suffer from low self-esteem. Narrow nails can be found on people who suffer from fatigue.

Almond or Oblong Nails

These are lovely nails to have, as these subjects will have a sweet disposition. They do all in their power to help others in distress. They also love animals. Their nature is not to be confrontational, but to placate and help others in life.

They have a healthy constitution, but they could have a tendency to food allergies when older. Diabetes is a possibility here, too.

Fan Shaped Nails

The owners of these shaped nails have a nervous disposition and their energy and drive can be used up quickly. Even as children, they will like to sleep a lot or have day-dreamy natures.

If very fan shaped and if the nails are red, these individuals can have psychological disorders. Another possibility is an addictive personality, so alcohol or drugs may be a problem at some point in their lives.

Watch Glass or Hippocratic Nails

These nails look like the glass cover of an old-fashioned pocket watch, as they are convex, sometimes even lifting from the beds at the sides. This person is mild mannered, easy to get along with, and makes a fair and easy-going boss in the workplace.

Their owners have a tendency toward respiratory problems, and in days gone by, this was a classic formation for those with tuberculosis. If this formation is present in people who smoke, there is an elevated risk of an early death, often as a result of lung cancer. Asthma can be another condition, as can cirrhosis of the liver, sarcoidosis, emphysema, and chronic bronchitis.

Sasha once told me a story about nails like these. She was sitting in a book store doing short readings in order to promote her own palmistry book, when a young woman who was the picture of health sat down opposite her. The moment Sasha saw her hands, she noticed the woman's watch glass nails. Sasha commented that a half-century ago, those nails would immediately alert a doctor that the patient had tuberculosis. The young lady answered she had recently spent several weeks in a special hospital, after catching TB while traveling in India!

Long Nails

This doesn't refer to people who happen to have grown their nails long; it's the length of the nail that's still on the nail bed.

These types have good imaginations, but if the nail is too long, they can live in a world of their own. Often these people will be interested in computer games and similar hobbies, and prefer to be engrossed in such pursuits rather than interact with others. The overall personality is pleasant, but they can lack drive and ambition, as they take everything at a leisurely pace. They lack vigor and could suffer with their backs and upper torso.

Small Nails

Those who have small child-like nails are exacting and shrewd, especially when female. They will love things to be in order and want everything spic and span. Unfortunately, they have a critical nature and can nag or nitpick, and they will never forget if they have been wronged. Their wit is sharp and they may delight in making their opinions known. They do have good common sense, though, and will assess situations very quickly.

As they can be highly strung, their nerves may be a problem, and lack of sleep can make them irritable. Rest is important, even taking small catnaps if necessary.

Fingernail Color

This can give information about the character of a person, their vigor—or lack of it—and their current state of health.

Medium Pink

This is the best color to have. It shows quick mental appreciation and an affectionate nature. These individuals are well balanced and friendly.

Reddish

The people with this color will have a strong sex drive and be highly tactile, but could have intense bouts of anger and high blood pressure. Their tolerance levels are low and they are constantly seeking new thrills.

Blue Tinge

Often these individuals will have poor circulation and feel the cold, so they are better suited to warmer climes. Their nature is slightly standoffish, and they can be cold in love because they hide their feelings, therefore making it hard for their partners to understand them.

Yellow Tinge

The owners of this type of nail may have problems with their liver. They should drink plenty of water and keep their alcohol intake low. They are not great sleepers and can wake up intermittently through the night, so they are often tired.

Whitish Grey

This can be an indication of circulatory problems, and often the hands will feel cold and clammy to the touch. These people can also suffer with pains in their joints, shoulders, and back when older.

Opaque Nails

White opaque nails with a dark banding at the top of the nail can often depict diabetes.

The Moons

The moons are a crescent-shaped formation that is a visible part of the nail matrix, and they have much to say about the client's constitution. Strangely, the moons are often absent on the Apollo finger, but they are almost always present on the thumb.

Normal Moons

A normal moon is a pale pink arc on the base of all the fingernails, and this signifies good blood pressure and circulation. The owner will be even-tempered and easy to get along with.

Blue Moons

When the moons have a blue line hugging them, this will signify bad circulation and sometimes chilblains.

No Moons

This can be a sign of blood pressure and circulatory problems. If there is no moon on the Mercury fingernail, the owner could suffer from lower back conditions, possibly as the result of an accident. If the moon is absent on the Apollo finger, creaky knees and joints could be a problem.

Over-Large Moons

This can be indicative of an overactive heart and an excitable temper. This owner will not take stress very well and can live on adrenalin. They are not easy to live with, as their standards are sometimes unattainable.

Changing Moons

If the moons suddenly change by enlarging or disappearing, then this can represent heart problems.

Blue/Grey Arc on Moons

Sometimes there may be a bluish or grey arc sitting on top of the moon, and the fingers feel cold or clammy. This is another sign of poor circulation. It seems to be more common in people who have the astrological sign of Aquarius.

Absent Moon on the Mercury Fingernail

This is quite common to see and the owners of this formation will usually suffer with lower back problems such as a slipped disc, usually caused by an accident when they were younger.

Fingernails and Health

When looking at the nails for health, it is important to stress that you must not frighten your clients when faced with the possibility of potentially serious problems. In my thirty years as a palmist, I have helped quite a few people to address their health issues, some of which they have known about, and some not. I have even saved lives. Only experience can teach the techniques of reading palms, and the first thing to learn is that you must be very careful about what you say, especially if you are at all unsure about the matter at hand—better to stay silent than to speculate.

However, if you feel sure, first gently ask the client if they have seen a doctor recently. If their answer is no, then you must decide whether to impart any information. This is the time that prior professional training in consulting and handling people shows its real need. It is not enough to cross fingers and hope that the client is an understanding type; you have as much responsibility as any doctor to your client, and if you presume to impart seriously disturbing information, you should be fully capable of handling any outcome. This skill does not come automatically, it has to be learned. Please speak in a calm, positive, and reassuring way, and perhaps suggest they go to see their doctor for a general checkup.

Fluted or Beaded Nails

Fluted nails can be a sign of rheumatoid arthritis, rheumatic disorders, and skin conditions such as eczema and acne. These tend to be seen on older hands, where the nail is often thickened and whitish in places.

Spoon Shaped Nails

When we see this on the fingernail, we know that the person is either suffering from a lack of nutrition or may have had some recent trauma. This formation can also indicate an underactive thyroid. In more serious cases, there might be brain damage or even something that has caused amnesia at some time in the past.

Pitted Nails

Skin diseases such as alopecia, dermatitis, and psoriasis cause this formation. If the nail has just one or two deep purple pits, this can mean the person has recently had a shock to the system.

Beau Lines or "Sea Waves"

Beau lines are like ridges or waves on the nail and they tell of a recent nail injury, a health condition, or that the person has suffered a shock. On one hand, this can signify a serious condition such as a heart attack, malnutrition, or trauma. They can also be left after a serious bout of influenza, an injury as a result of an accident, or a slipped disc or other spinal problems—in fact anything else that is memorable. It could be a relationship break-up, losing a job, a financial collapse, or a very stressful time in general.

Lateral Wave Lines

If these lateral dents and ridges are stacked up, we know the owner has been in a state of repeated shock or trauma and could be very fragile. When found on the thumb of females, in multiple ridges, there could be hormonal or menstrual problems present. Another theory is there could be an imbalance with heart rhythms.

Central Ridges

When you see this formation on the nails, you will know the person will have been through a very bad time, as it represents repeated traumas and sometime a huge shock to the system. Arterial disease could also be present, or there could have been severe malnutrition or vitamin deficiency.

Fir-Tree Nails

Sometimes a raised ridge ends in an effect that slightly raises part of the nail end from the bed. The effect looks like a fir-tree at the end of the nail. This is a classic indication of heart trouble, often on the hands of an older person.

Mee Lines

White lines running horizontally across the nail are usually a clear sign of a recent trauma.

Nail Separation

When the nail starts to separate from the nail bed, it can denote anaemia or thyroid problems, or a fungal disease. This can sometimes arise after a bad reaction to drugs. Nail damage caused by false nails can also look similar, so it is best to ask the client about this first.

Terry's Nails

Named after Dr. Richard Terry, who completed a study of this condition in the 1950s, Terry's nails show the tips of the nails to be opaque with a darker band on the upper part of the nail. This can indicate heart failure, diabetes, liver disease, and malnutrition and kidney problems.

Yellow Nails

This condition will be easy to spot, because of the color. The person might be suffering with diabetes, jaundice, nerve injury, or bronchitis. One or two discolored nails might be the result of smoking, most likely the Jupiter and Saturn fingernails.

Brown Lined Nails

This can be quite a serious condition, but do check the person has not had a blow to the nail. If a brown or bluish line is seen running down the nail, this can indicate breast cancer, Addison's disease, melanoma, or trauma.

Ridged Nails

Vertical ridges on the nails are usually harmless, and often nothing more than old age creeping up on the client. Sometime the nail can split, so a good nail restoring cream should be recommended. There could be a need to increase foods such as brown rice, sunflower seeds, or sweet potatoes. Perhaps a small iron deficiency might be present, and often the owner will suffer from rheumatism or arthritis. These are all situations that arise from getting older and poor nutrition.

One Ridge Standing Out

Sometimes the nails as a whole aren't ridged, but there could be a couple of ridges that stand out on one or two nails. This suggests some kind of trauma to a bone or a muscle, and cartilage, ligaments and tendons surrounding it. The actual finger will often point to the area in question. For instance, a problem with the neck or spine will show up on the thumb and/or Jupiter finger. Shoulders, hips, pelvis, and central and lower spine will show up on the Saturn finger. Arms and legs will show up on the Apollo fingernail, and then ankles, wrists, hands, and feet on the Mercury finger.

Black Spots

Black spots or small black smudgings on the nails can indicate impurities in the blood or a fungal infection.

Brittle Nails

Sometimes the nails will split and break before they are fully grown. It's a good idea to advise the person to wear rubber gloves when doing domestic chores or when handling bleach. If the nails are very pale, the person could be anemic. As mentioned before, brittle nails can also be caused by the subject's finances being out of control.

Reddish-Brown Spots

When a person has brawny, reddish pits or marks on the nail, this is an indication of a folic acid deficiency or a lack of vitamin C.

Thin Black Lines

This can be quite a serious condition and it's one that's not often seen, but when present, it may indicate heart disease.

White Spots

White flecks or spots on the nails are a very common sight and they're usually harmless, often caused by blows that damage the nail to create this formation. In traditional palmistry, this can also indicate a shortage of calcium and zinc in the diet, but nowadays there is controversy about this theory. Sasha says this tends to be a common sight at the end of winter, so it seems to be partly caused by spending a lot of time indoors.

Arched White Line

Curved white lines can signify metal poisoning, e.g. lead.

Soft Nails/ Thin Nails

Soft, thin nails can denote malnutrition, endocrine problems, and chronic arthritis.

14

The Thumb—
Venus on the Hand

The thumb has about the same importance on the hand as the nose on your face. The thumb represents love, logic, and willpower.

- Love is represented by the base of the thumb, which becomes the Mount of Venus.

- Logic is represented by the lower phalange of the thumb.

- Willpower is represented by the top phalange, namely, the nail portion of the thumb.

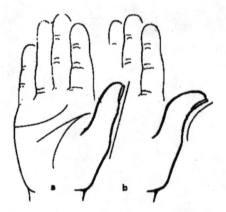

Stiff-Jointed Thumb (a)

Owners of a stiff-jointed thumb will be less flexible and more rigid in their beliefs, and they will take a lot of persuasion when asked to try something new. These people are less extravagant than those who have the supple-jointed thumb. The nearer the thumb clings to the side of the hand, especially if it cramps the palm, the more these subjects are inclined to seek financial security.

Those who are a little careful with money have thumbs that sit more closely and higher up on the hand. These types will also find it hard to move on from tradition, i.e., religious or political beliefs. They are also private individuals.

Supple or Flexible Thumb (b)

This represents a nature that is pliable and adaptable to others. Such subjects are broad-minded and often unconventional. The supple-jointed thumb also denotes generosity of mind, both in thought and money, and indicates a forgiving nature. These people are more extravagant than those who have the straight, firm-jointed thumb (a). Supple thumbed owners are impulsive and make instant decisions, often to be regretted later. They are fun, chatty, and like "will-o'-the-wisps," so you're never bored in their company.

Straight Thumb (a)

What you see is what you get. They are kind hearted and hate to foist things upon others, so they don't make good sales people. They need plenty of peace and quiet to recharge their batteries and sometimes prefer to work solo to get out of the rat race. As they are self-contained, they won't mind being alone for days on end, as they love space to think, dream, and be independent.

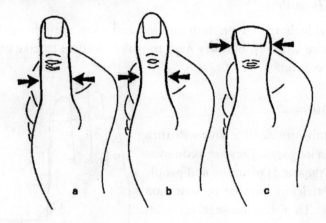

The Waisted Thumb (b)

To a great extent, these individuals rely on their instincts. Often they will do things on the spur of the moment, hoping that fate will give them a helping hand.

The Clubbed Thumb (the Murderer's Thumb) (c)

Through the centuries of palmistry, the clubbed thumb has been controversial. It is also called the elementary thumb. My long-dead grandmother would say that some of the thumbs she had seen looked as though they had been hit with a ten-pound lump hammer. If the rest of the fingers were markedly different, this formation would look out of place on the hand. These people seem to be somewhat resentful, possibly with good reason.

Flat Flexible Thumb

These types are often highly strung and will live on their nerves. Their constitutions are often delicate and they suffer from small and annoying health problems. Having a nervous disposition can hold them back from their true potential, so they will often be late starters.

Stiff Flat Thumb

These individuals are Victorian in outlook and a law unto themselves. They are hard workers, but they need to make an effort to take others into consideration.

Actor's Thumb

These thumbs are flexible and will turn back quite a long way. They are a common feature on the hands of actors and people who have to learn lines or presentation techniques. They can be seen on sales people and lecturers. Sometimes, these types can be rather full of themselves.

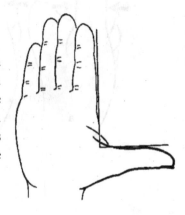

The Angles of the Thumb

When looking at a person's hand, it is wise to take stock of the way it opens; therefore, the space between the Jupiter finger and the thumb is of great importance.

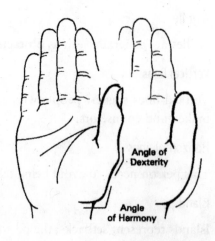

When thumbs sit high on the palm, are placed close to the Jupiter finger, and are rigid, these types will have tunnel vision and unbending opinions. They can often be a law unto themselves.

THUMB PHALANGES

Look for the following features and marks on the thumb phalanges.

A star

A star formation on the top phalange suggests a manipulative nature.

A cross

This person is easily led.

A triangle

A triangle is an exceptionally fortunate mark that represents academic types who shine in philosophy and scientific work.

A square

A square suggests stubbornness, but this also involves a logical, reasoning mind.

A circle

A circle denotes strong powers of concentration and someone who is logical about most matters. This brings great success.

A grille

Grilles are generally seen as obstacles.

Vertical lines

Vertical lines suggest people who can see both sides of the story and make good counselors.

Horizontal lines

This person needs to avoid being taken in by unscrupulous people.

Islands

Islands represent setbacks; the person ought to focus on his own needs and not allow others to walk all over him.

part five

SPECIAL MARKINGS

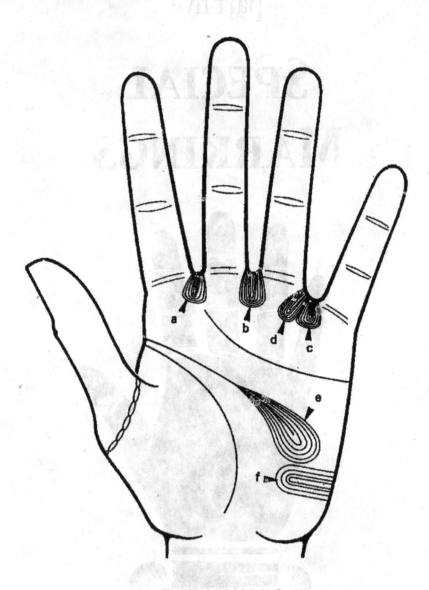

PALMAR LOOPS A–F

15

Palmar Loops

Palmar dermatoglyphics are much the same as fingerprints, in that they are formed when the person is still in the womb, and they don't change through life in the way that lines do.

However, they can break down into "string of pearls" formations if the person becomes ill or if they become addicted to something.

Palmar loops can give us a fascinating glimpse into a person's character.

The Rajah Loop (see a)

This formation occurs between the Jupiter and Saturn finger and is quite rare. In Vedic palmistry, the person who is fortunate enough to have this is supposed to have a charmed life and is blessed with charisma, good looks, power, and kudos. It can also mean high breeding with royal connections, or the person might have descended from important and powerful people. The person will have a regal look and good bearing, with fine taste in furnishings and food. When these people enter a room, there will be an air of importance about them, and they will certainly have the "X factor."

I asked Sasha if she had any good stories about the rajah loop, as I had never seen one in my career, and what she told me was fascinating:

I was working at a large London festival of mind, body and spirit, where you do one reading after another fairly quickly. One day, two handsome, youngish men, both with the look of Seve Ballesteros about them, sat down together in front of me, although only one of them had booked a reading. They were so alike they were clearly brothers. My client thrust his hands out and after a quick look at the back of his hands and his fingernails, I turned his hand over and saw a rajah loop on each palm. Seeing one rajah loop is rare, but seeing two is almost unheard of. I glanced up and told my client he must have royal blood running in his veins. His eyebrows shot up and he said he and his brother were Dukes of Braganza, which meant they were members of the Portuguese royal family. I asked if I could see the other brother's hand and sure enough, he also carried a rajah loop on each hand.

The Loop of Serious Intent (see b)

This is located between the Apollo and Saturn fingers. The owners will be studious, strong minded, and reliable. They take life very seriously and try to make the best of themselves, especially in education. There will be a quest for knowledge, and the more of it the better. My grandmother told me that this formation on the palm would rarely see its owner suffer with senile dementia, as their mind stays forever young and alert.

The Loop of Humor (see c)

This fits between the Mercury and Apollo fingers. These people are fun loving, mischievous, and have a naughty sense of the ridiculous. They can cheer people up and bring a light-hearted atmosphere to any gathering. If the loop is high up on the hand, the owners will love animals and often subscribe to animal charities and events. If the loop has a central whorl, they are gifted in foreign languages and could find work as interpreters or even live abroad.

The Loop of Style or the Vanity Loop (see d)

This will be side by side with the loop of humor, between the Mercury and Apollo fingers. Although it has been known in the past as a sign of self interest and vanity, modern day palmists tend to look on this as people with style who will like to look after themselves and who have a good eye for fashion, color, and interior design and decorating. Their creative streak is strong and they are inventive. On an artistic hand, the owner will probably have a career in fashion and design.

The Loop of Memory (see e)

This is found at the end of the head line and is usually very distinctive and quite large. The owner will have a memory like an elephant and will keep details from long ago stored in his head like a computer. If they are shown something just once, they will get the hang of it and never forget the procedure. They remember names and addresses of years gone by, and have the knack of clever and witty conversation. However, they can bear a grudge, as even negative thoughts will get stored away and never be forgotten.

The Loop of Imagination (see f)

This loop sits between the Luna Mount and the Mount of Mars, linking with psychic skills and imagination. These people will tend to rely on their own judgment, their motto being carpe diem . . . seize the day!

They have an uncanny knack of reading your mind and may have strong feelings of world events before they happen, especially if the loop has a whorl inside. Loops in the Luna area show a love of nature and outdoor pursuits like camping, canoeing, skiing, and hiking.

16

The Rascettes

The rascettes are also known as the Rascettes of Venus, or the magic bracelets.

The Rascettes of Venus are found on the inside of the hand on the wrist, and they usually contain three lines (a). They can also be found arching upward (b).

Each unbroken line is supposed to give its owner around thirty years of life. Sometimes a fourth line will be clearly visible, which foretells a very long life.

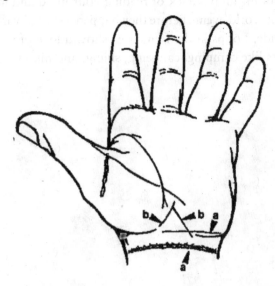

Arched Rascette

An arched rascette can sometimes be a sign of hard work and difficulties.

Triangular Rascette

A triangular rascette is not a good omen, as it can signify gynecological problems for a female and possibly a hysterectomy at some time in the future or the past. If on a male hand, prostate trouble could be an issue. If the line is inflamed, the situation is current. If the triangle is smaller, then continence might be a problem.

Chained Rascette

A chained rascette is often the sign of ongoing family difficulties and health problems. The owner will tend to be tired and run down.

Fragmented Rascettes

Fragmented rascettes show a lack of foresight, ambition, and a lack of organizational abilities. These types will leave things to the last minute.

Grilled Rascettes

Grilled rascettes are common on the hand and can mean obstacles are in place. If twinned with an arched rascette, the diagnosis for female health might be complicated and deeper investigation may be needed. Scans or blood tests will be on the agenda.

- A cross in the rascette is usually an ill omen and can be a warning to watch for upsets and accidents. If on the nondominant hand, this may have already happened. If the cross is surrounded by a square, the subject will be protected against disaster.

- Ascending lines between each of the rascettes are positive signs because these people are doing well in their lives and making good progress.

- A square in the rascette area means the person has spiritual protection and real luck. They may live off the beaten track, or travel to unusual places, and they tend to live a charmed life.

- An eight-pointed star in the rascette is a very good omen, as it means the owner could see or experience something truly wonderful in their lives, often of a spiritual nature such as an angel, UFO, etc.

17

The Mouse

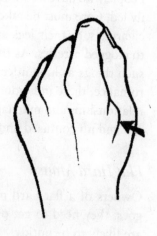

Look at the back of the hand and close the thumb; you will see a pad of flesh on the hand next to the lower end of the thumb. In Vedic palmistry, this was studied closely to judge the vitality of the person. It can show the state of the person's lung functions and whether there are any respiratory problems. The Mouse is also known as the Vault.

Round Firm Mouse

Those with a round firm mouse have strong vitality and resistance to illness, with strong bones and muscles. They will be driven, boisterous, brave, and full of optimism. They love to travel and get off the beaten track and may enjoy hunting, fishing, and camping in remote places. They make good soldiers or athletic teachers. Nothing will faze them, and they will enjoy life to the fullest. In matters of love, these types don't want a homebody, but a companion who is on the same level as them. Their libido will be high and sex will be very important. They will be too busy conquering the world to think much about their spiritual life.

Medium Mouse

Those who have a medium sized mouse are balanced individuals who will have a wide variety of interests. Their energy levels are normal, so they enjoy quiet and active times. They are good listeners and usually full of fun. As they get older, the owners will start to dwell on the bigger picture and will become seekers of knowledge. These subjects enjoy good health and usually have a long and happy life, providing they do things in moderation. In matters of the heart, communication will be very important to them. They are romantic and devoted, loving to be wined and dined, and will need a romantic partner to complete their lives.

Soft Mouse

People who have a soft or flaccid mouse tend to be weak-willed and easily led. Care must be taken with the lungs and they should never smoke cigarettes, as their legs and veins will pose a problem in later life, due to clogged arteries. As their lungs can be weak, they could suffer from such things as lung infections, bronchitis, emphysema, and asthma. In romance, these individuals make many mistakes and often have failed relationships and marriages because they leap before they look, so they can end up confused and lonely in later life.

Flat Hard Mouse

Owners of a flat hard mouse have much to learn, and, as the saying goes, they need to get out more! They have little physical energy and are likely to be untidy.

18

Mystic Markings

The hand holds many markings that contain secrets from ancient palmistry. To be fair, some are no more than superstitions handed down from the generations of gypsies, soothsayers, and mystics, but many are uncannily accurate, as I have discovered in over thirty years as a working palmist.

Initials are often placed in the hands, and if an initial is on the nondominant palm, then this is someone the subject already knows. However, when the initial is on the future palm, then this person has yet to come in to the client's life.

The Square

A square placed anywhere in the palm can be a mark of protection, especially if there is a cross within it. This can denote an accident that could have been worse than it was, or a time when the person's life was saved. The square can also represent talent for the owner, but they may lack courage to put their talents into action, so you might need to encourage them with this.

The Ring of Solomon (c)

The Ring of Solomon is found in a semicircle at the base of the Jupiter finger. It is rare and considered to be very lucky. This formation tells us that the owner is psychic and will be gifted in all aspects of the occult and divination. Good luck and prosperity will bring happiness to the individual, who will always be in the right place at the right time.

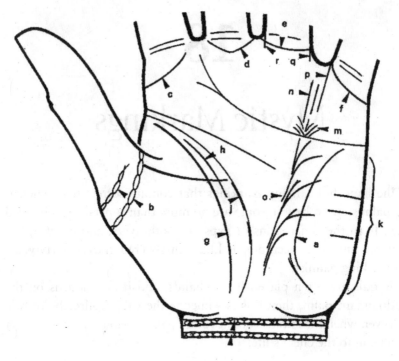

The Ring of Saturn (d)

The Ring of Saturn sits just below the Saturn finger in a semi-circle. This is not a good thing to see, as it can portend difficulties for the owner. Common sense will not always be present and psychological problems could plague the person, hindering future judgement and possible future success.

The Ring of Apollo (e)

When this configuration is in place, it can indicate restricted areas of life associated with Apollo, which means the person is going through a time of deep unhappiness within the family and other personal relationships. With effort, they can change their lives and bring harmony.

The Ring of Mercury (j)

This can often be a sign that the subject will become a widow or widower. This line was present on Sasha's hand while she was living with her first husband; he then died of cancer. It faded after she married for a second time.

It is always worth bearing in mind that the lines on the hand can change, and they can do so quite rapidly if the individual alters their way of going about things. Even unlucky marks, especially negative health lines, can miraculously disappear when the person turns over a new leaf or changes to a healthier and more active lifestyle.

Marks on the Hand

There are many marks that can appear independently on a palm or as part of a line. Each has a different meaning, and while it's impossible to remember them all, you can use this book to refer back to whenever you come across one of these. Here is a brief rundown of some of their meanings. Some of these marks stand alone on the hand, while others will be attached to a line on the hand.

Star

This can signify a recent shock or problem, especially if the star is reddish in color. In Vedic palmistry, it can also be a sacred mark if found on certain areas of the hand. If, for instance, it is present in the quadrangle, the owner will be truly blessed.

Square

This means protection or restriction, depending upon the position of the square. For instance, a square on the heart line means the person's emotions or love life aren't flowing freely or happily. A square on a mount can represent protection from harm in whatever that mount represents.

Grille

A stand-alone mark that signifies severe trauma to some part of the body. For example, it will show up after an operation, but then fade away somewhat when the person recovers from the problem.

Pentagram

This is a rare sign of psychic or magical gifts. Often, the client can be a Wiccan witch if they have this mark.

Triangle or Half Diamond

When independent, this indicates talent, luck, and inheritance. If the triangle is suspended under the head line however, it means the person has gone through, is going through, or will go through a feeling of imprisonment. This may be due to being stuck in an unpleasant job or a negative relationship. It can indicate an actual prison sentence.

Flag

A flag on the life line in Vedic palmistry can sometimes signify an inheritance. Where the flag is placed should give an indication of timing.

Cross

This is usually considered a negative sign in Vedic palmistry, such as accidents and misfortunes. In Western palmistry, if this is seen on the Luna or Neptune mount, protection can be given for sea travel and seasickness. On the Apollo mount, it can mean a windfall.

Cross in a Box

The cross represents a severe problem or danger, but the box shows the subject will be (or has been) protected from the worst effects. This configuration will often be present in life or death situations.

Circle

A circle is a rare sign and there can be some controversy with palmists. In Vedic palmistry it is a good omen, but in traditional palmistry, it means the opposite.

Chains and Islands

These always represent a string of bad luck, ill health, and obstacles for the owner. Read the chapters on the lines to see what these mean in each case.

Slanting Line

Usually a slanting line crosses a major or a minor line. It can represent disruption in the individual's life, or it can denote a time when something breaks up completely. If the line is intermittent or dashed, the owner could be having start-stop scenarios.

Tassels

These can appear at the ends of the lines and show a weakening of that part of the person's body and vitality, sometimes due to illness or old age. For instance, a tassel on the head line can denote dementia, or if it is seen at the end of the life line, the person could have physical difficulties in later life.

Fork

This represents a parting of the ways.

Multiple Lines

This formation dissipates the strength of the line, which then splits itself into small parts. It can actually be a good thing, such as when it appears on the fate lines signifying self-employment. Because there are multiple lines, the owner could have many irons in the fire, but will have to soldier on alone. Eventually their hard work will pay off.

Uplifting Lines

Lines that rise up from the major lines denote an upswing in the individual's circumstances, so this is always a fortunate thing to see.

Down Slope Lines

Lines that droop down from some of the major lines can be a negative configuration for the owner's life.

Wavy Lines

Waves on the line, or wavy lines around it, denote some form of weakness. It might be due to bad health, insomnia, or aspects of the person's work that are causing problems at the time of the reading.

Warts, Moles, Marks, and Scars

You won't see an abundance of moles on the palm side of the hands, but when you do, they represent blocks of some sort, stopping the owner's progress. If there is a mole on the Mount of Venus, the subject could be having relationship problems. Warts are more common, and they also denote restrictions. Look at where they are placed on the hand to find the answers. When moles, warts, and scars are seen on the back of the hand, it could be someone else who is holding the person back. If the scars are old, it could be a past-life issue.

Red Patches

Redness on one finger or one particular area of the hand shows a temporary feeling of frustration due to the behavior of others or life in general. Check the finger in question or the area of the hand to see what's going on. If there is a red patch on a woman's palm on the percussion side of the hand, there might be hormonal problems or she could be going through the change of life. If the Neptune mount is red, there could be urinary infections or menstruation upsets. Often when the problems have subsided, the color will go back to normal.

part six

OUT OF YOUR HANDS

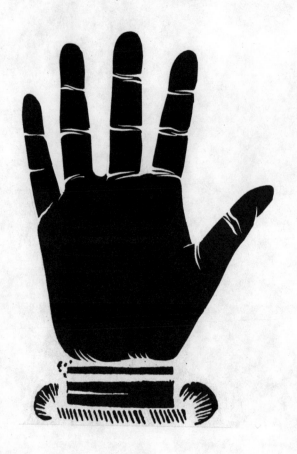

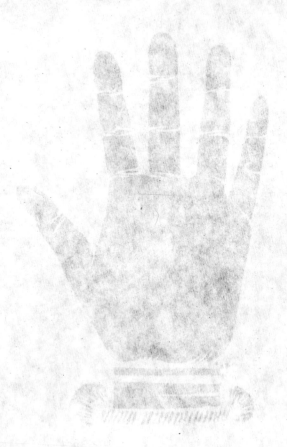

19

Relationship Styles

The hand reveals much more than character traits and fate. From out of our hands come insights into relationships, health, and spirituality. Let us consider first what the hand can tell us about relationships.

The Faithful Partner

Those who have earthy hands with little or no spaces between the fingers usually take things very seriously and will stick to a partner for life. A constant hand will have broad nails and fingers that can be a little inflexible. Study the head line to make sure there are no erratic lines present. A clear head line indicates a focused type of individual. The heart line should slope gently, and it should be free of fissures or erratic marks. If the line is a healthy pink color with no tassels, the subject will be forgiving and nurturing.

The Deceptive Partner

In my career as a palmist, I have discovered the birth signs that find it hardest to settle down can be Sagittarius and Aries. Usually, they will have a typical fire hand (short fingers and a longer palm) and the hand will be firm and slightly red. Often, the Plain of Mars will be under-developed and the concavity a little deep. Fire palms are passionate, and they like variety, so they can become bored when in a steady relationship. They take longer to mature and find true love, so they break many hearts along the way. When the Mount of Venus is over-developed and has a red tinge, the libido will be very high. The heart line will be a deeper red and might have chains and scratchy marks over it. Look under the

Mercury finger for the attachment lines to see how many conquests there are, and if there are forked lines, a divorce might already have occurred. The Mercury finger could incline sharply toward the Apollo finger, indicating a deceptive nature.

The Unsure Partner

This type of palm can either be Air or Water, and the Pisces or Gemini signs fall into this category. They yearn for love and a stable relationship but can make bad choices because their hearts rule their heads. The Mount of Venus will be quite rounded, but perhaps a little flaccid. The fingers are long and pointed, which represents their dreamy and unrealistic nature. They seek ideal love that can be found only in books, so their heart line can have breaks and fissures, while the Girdle of Venus will be fragmented. Many will end up having a number of lovers, not through promiscuity, but through failed relationships or a continued search for something worthwhile. These types usually go through one or two divorces, so study the relationship lines on the Mercury Mount. Also look at the head line, because it could be bitty and broken, showing that the subject moves around and sets up home with one partner after another.

The Bossy and Abusive Partner

These types usually belong to the Fire and Air hands, and I have seen the signs more than once on Water hands. The Jupiter finger could have extra length and be wider than the other fingers. If the Lower Mars Mount is overdeveloped, the subject may have the unpleasant trait of lashing out both verbally and physically. A clubbed thumb is not a good thing to see, as it represents a quick, violent temper and child-like tantrums and sulks. If the head line is strong, red, and chained, the individuals may have a sadistic nature with a real need to control their partners, children, siblings, and parents. Check if the hand is right for the body and not too short for the height or the makeup of the individual. The Mount of Venus could look too pronounced and overly red.

The Weird Partner

Some of the Water hands can fall into this category, as they have secretive personalities, while small hands that are a little fiery can also suggest a strange nature.

Attachment Lines

Lines called attachment lines concern love relationships, marriage-type partnerships, actual marriages, and important love affairs. Hands can't show marriage certificates or divorce paperwork, but they do signify emotional attachments, hence the name "attachment lines."

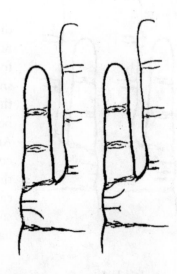

So, if you want to see how many marriages or serious relationships a person has had, or will have, you need to look closely at the percussion side of the hand between the heart line and the Mercury finger. These lines may be easier to read if you bend the Mercury finger slightly forward and look at the lines that enter the hand from the percussion side, on the area between the finger and the heart line.

Widows and Widowers

One theory is that a line that loops down to touch the heart line can sometimes indicate widowhood. Other palmists say this drooping line has nothing to do with widowhood, as it merely shows the client is being "put upon" by his or her partner. Some say that the "widow line" runs upward under the Mercury finger and "cups" the base of the finger. Attachment lines change direction fairly quickly, so if someone loses a partner who made them unhappy, and subsequently gets over the death easily and possibly moves on to another partner, the hand will change. The general feeling is that you should say very little on this subject, unless you know for certain that your client has already lost a partner through death or if the client already knows that their partner isn't likely to live much longer.

Difficulties in Relationships

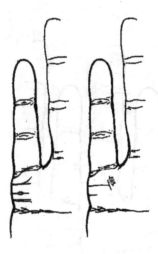

A forked attachment line can indicate a split in the relationship, and possibly an actual divorce. If a line is faint and scratchy, the relationship will be undecided and difficult for the person. Sometimes you can see a small purple dot on a relationship line, and this does not auger well, as there might be violence or hardship within the union. An island on a relationship line can mean constant bickering between the couple, and they could part in time. The island can indicate another possibility, which is that the subject's partner is not in good health or is handicapped in some way.

Multiple Lines

Sometimes when reading a hand, you can see three lines: widowhood, divorce, and relationship blips. The person might have gone through all three experiences, so this is a case of having the confidence to tactfully ask your client if this has happened to them.

Happy Marriages

When someone has been blessed with a loving marriage or relationship, there will be a straight, strong unbroken line. When a person is to be truly god blessed in marriage to a soul mate, there will be a straight line with another one tightly hugging it from below. In old-fashioned gypsy palmistry, this is called "spooning," and it's similar to the way that lovers cuddle into each other like teaspoons lying in a drawer. It is really rare to see this formation, and I have witnessed it only about five times in my working life as a palmist.

Child Lines

Child lines are found at the base of the Mercury mount, and they run downward, cutting through the attachment lines.

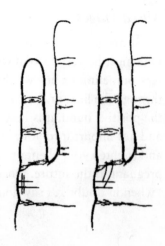

Traditionally, it is said that straight lines represent boys and slanting lines signify girls. I don't find this view completely accurate, and I can find myself being let down by the analysis. For instance, I have four straight lines, which would indicate sons, when in actual fact, I have just one child, a daughter. However, I once read for a very beautiful blond woman with the figure of a goddess. She had seven straight lines on her hand and my common sense told me not make a fool of myself by asking if she had seven sons! Later she revealed she had three sets of twin boys and had just had another baby boy. Even to my ears, it sounded too fantastic to be true, but it can happen!

Sasha says that multiple lines in this area can denote someone who loves children and looks after them for others, or someone who runs scout groups or teaches dance or sports to children. Another type that she has often come across is someone who has a deep affection for animals. I certainly love animals and have always kept pets, and there are many wild animals that come to my garden for love, attention, and food.

Sickness on the Child Lines

If an island is present on a children's line, the child could be prone to ill health. If there is a purple dot, it can be more sinister, as the child could be sexually abused or ill treated and bullied. One often wonders if the parent is responsible for this or if someone else is perpetrating the deed without the parents' knowledge. It is a difficult situation to approach and in my reading, I would just hint that a child might need protecting and for the parent to be watchful of negative people around their children.

Miscarriages

These are generally found on the minor hand rather than the major one. One must be very careful when speaking to a woman about these matters. Sometimes a line will be faint and there could be a cross formation through the line, or the line may be fractured and in bits. When seen on the positive hand, it is best for you to keep that knowledge to yourself and not impart it to your client. You might make an incorrect analysis and frighten your client or cause them unnecessary stress if they become pregnant in the future. Once again, the old saying comes to mind that, "when in doubt . . . say nought!"

20

Spiritual and
Psychic Palmistry

Many people love to hear about their psychic potential, and there are various indications of this in the hand. Information about this aspect of life has, in part, been handed down through my family, but also from esteemed palmists whom I have met and from observing thousands of palms over the years.

Full Hand

When there are many lines in the palm, the person had a full life and he will experience difficult lessons, especially if the mounts of the hand are well formed. This brings wisdom, empathy, and great spiritual understanding. Their souls will be wise, and often they will help younger souls to reach a steadier pathway.

Widely Spaced Fingers

Individuals that have well spaced fingers have minds open to all things spiritual and esoteric.

Large Neptune Mount

The Neptune mount sits just above the wrists, and if it is very round and plump the owner will be deep thinking and very tuned in to the energies of the planet. I have often seen this formation on the hands of Wiccan witches and psychics. The animal kingdom will be important to them, and they love to be outside to soak up the vibration of their planet. They can sense impending disasters and predict where they will happen.

Large Luna Mount

Those whose fate lines start on Luna are guided by fate and they are keen to help others. Psychic palmists think these people are reincarnated for a special reason. On a scientific hand, these folks may invent something to help mankind. When seen on a medical hand, the owners will have been given pioneering skills to help dispel disease. A large Luna mount also represents psychic ability and a deep connection to moon magic.

The Phalanges

Vertical lines running up through the phalanges relate to subjects who work on improving their souls and their Karma. The ascending lines through the phalanges show that the owner has quite a hard life, but they gain much wisdom and knowledge from their experiences. They can uplift others and give hope to the desperate. If there is a strong medical striata on the Mount of Mercury, the owner will be interested in healing, crystals, and flower remedies.

Sloping Head Line

When the head line slopes toward the percussion side of the palm, the owners will be spiritual. They seek knowledge through books, meditation, and inward reflection. When the head line is too long or curved, these folk tend to have their heads in the air, seeking out gurus or other religious leaders to buoy up their faith. The ideas of others exert too much influence on them, and they may slavishly follow others rather than working things out for themselves.

Dead straight head lines suggest individuals who aren't interested in religion or spirituality. They will concentrate more on science, business, money, travel, their appearance, their status, their homes, antiques, possessions, or any number of other worldly matters.

Inner Life Line

Sometimes the hand will look as if it has an inner and outer life line. I have given the practical meaning to this earlier in the book, but I also believe the inner life line or "shadow line" on the perimeters of the Mount of Venus can tell us that the person has higher levels of protection. The subject could have a guardian angel or a spiritual guide. If the protection line starts from childhood, it can show the person's youth has been checkered and spiritual guardianship has been needed. If the line appears later down in the palm, the owner will have lived through some form of crisis or even a life-and-death situation, especially if there are grilles, gaps, or crosses on the line.

Mercury Line, Health Line, Via Hepatica

There are several lines that can run up the hand toward the Mercury finger, and these can have a variety of names, depending upon the different styles of palmistry. These lines can indicate health problems in the hands of the subject, but just as often, they denote an interest in health and healing, either in the context of conventional medicine or the complementary variety. If you see this, also look for the Medical Striata. A curved line anywhere in this area suggests a psychic ability. People who have this line on the nondominant hand will be born psychic, but they may not use their gift consciously. Those who have the line on the dominant hand will develop intuition at some point in their life, either deliberately or as a side effect of struggles during their lifetime. If there is a curved line somewhere in this area on both hands, the owners will make good use of their intuitive gifts.

The Mystic Cross

This should be placed in the middle of the Quadrangle, which is formed by the head line and the heart line, and the cross must be independent and not touching either of the lines. If you draw a line upward from the center of the cross, it should end between the Apollo and Saturn fingers.

Sometimes the Mystic Cross will be visible only on one hand, but it really should be apparent in both hands. This mark sits in the middle of the Quadrangle and is very rare, as it might be seen only in one in four hundred hands. The owner would do well in tarot, palmistry, or mediumistic work. This subject would be a very good judge of character.

This is the sign of the psychic or medium, and the owners will find it easy to link into the spirit world. Most of their lives will be closely linked to esoteric and holistic areas. If parents have a child with this fortunate sign, they should encourage the child to develop their skills at an early age. My own daughter, Leanna Greenaway, has this mark and has since gone on to write many books on different subjects linked to esoteric and Wiccan beliefs. From the age of three, she has been able to see angels, guides, and pets that have passed away. Owners of the Mystic Cross may also have a strange electrical energy, and their domestic appliances will break down quite frequently. Their auras are sensitive, so they get sudden electrical shocks from shopping carts or metal surfaces. Mystic Cross people can see the future in their dreams, and they can see others' auras.

The Kundalini

Mystic cross owners often experience the Kundalini, and here is a short explanation.

The Kundalini is a Vedic concept. The idea is that our spiritual strength lies at the base of the spine. Vedic scholars depict this as a snake that they call "the sleeping serpent." The energy rises up the body and threads its way through the chakras until it exits the crown chakra (top of the head). The vibration from the body then connects with spiritual energy called Prana. The person experiences a crackling or electrical energy racing up through the spine. Once this is over, the Kundalini settles down and a feeling of well-being or healing ensues.

21

Health and
Hand Textures

Hand texture informs the palmist about the character and the current health of the client. I must stress that palmists should never try to be a doctor and diagnose anything, but it can be helpful to warn a client in a very tactful way about health matters and suggest a visit to their doctor.

Hold the person's hand, turn the palm upward, and press the Mount of Venus and the other mounts on the hand with your forefinger. If these spring back quickly, this is a healthy hand.

Soft Hands

People with soft hands have a timid and quiet nature. They wish to please and have a gentle and forgiving soul. When reading for this type, it is wise to encourage them to have a little more backbone because others can push them around.

Sick people and the elderly can have this type of skin texture. There could be a need to assess their diet, as there could be a vitamin deficiency present. We often see this condition with vegans and vegetarians. In younger women, this shows when they are overdoing the dieting.

Silky Hands

There will be a definite sheen to this hand, which will make it look as if the person has just rubbed in hand cream. Those with firm hands will be clever. They think with their heads rather than their hearts, and their intellect will carry them through life. These types are outstanding in their goals and achievements. If the hand is silky and soft, the owner might be prone to insomnia.

Wet Palms (Palmar Hydrosis)

This can be a tricky thing to identify, as the person might just be nervous at having their palm read.

Sweating palms often run in families. A more sinister side can suggest thyroid and febrile illnesses, and sometimes injuries and heart problems.

Pale Hands

This person will lack motivation, or they might be anemic.

Red Hands

This suggests people with fiery natures who are quick thinking and restless. The client may suffer from cirrhosis, or in some cases from the results of heavy smoking.

Orange or Yellow Hands

I once saw this color on the hands of a person who was a health freak and ate vast quantities of carrots! If the person isn't poisoning their system with carrots, yellow skin can indicate jaundice.

Grey-Blue Hands

This indicates circulatory and heart problems.

Red mottles on the Luna Mounts

This may indicate gynecological problems, overactive thyroid, and high blood pressure.

Blue-White Hands

This is linked with poor circulation, and the person could feel more comfortable by living in a warmer climate. Sometimes there will be red or orange blotches present on the backs of the hand as well.

Pale Dry Hands

These people lack variety in their social life, or they may be dehydrated, or both.

Hard or "Wooden Hands"

Sometimes people who work on the land will have this type of palm, and they will be self-reliant and very tough. They will be critical of themselves and others, as they do not suffer fools gladly. If the person has a more sedentary job, their nature will be edgy, and they can sometimes have a cruel streak. They can have bad nerves, be worriers, and usually suffer from rheumatic problems in later life.